Research Agenda for Networked Cultural Heritage

THE GETTY
ART HISTORY
INFORMATION
PROGRAM

THE GETTY ART HISTORY INFORMATION PROGRAM

The mission of the Getty Art History
Information Program (AHIP) is to enhance
access to art and humanities information for
research and education through the use of
computer technology. In collaboration with
institutions and organizations internationally,
AHIP addresses the research needs, standards,
and practices that can bring the full benefits of
digitized information to the cultural heritage
community.

Copyright © 1996 The J. Paul Getty Trust
All rights reserved
Design: James Robie Design Associates
Printed in the United States
ISBN 0-89236-414-9

The Getty Art History Information Program
401 Wilshire Boulevard, Suite 1100
Santa Monica, California 90401-1455
Telephone: (310) 395-1025
Telefax: (310) 451-5570
Electronic mail: ahip@getty.edu
Internet (World Wide Web): http://www.ahip.getty.edu/ahip/home.html

CONTENTS

OVERVIEW AND DISCUSSION POINTS

David Bearman, Archives & Museum Informatics

PREFACE

In 1994 the Clinton Administration was developing policies for the National Information Infrastructure (NII) and seeking to make a business case for investing public money in it. Interests throughout the country, including those in the arts and humanities, were approached to help the Administration articulate the importance of supporting the information revolution for economic development, scientific and scholarly progress, and improvements in the quality of life. The Getty Art History Information Program (AHIP), with the American Council of Learned Societies and the Coalition for Networked Information, worked with scholars throughout the country to write a white paper entitled "Humanities and Arts on the Information Highways: A Profile," the early drafts of which were influential in shaping the Administration's Information Infrastructure Task Force Committee on Applications and Technology report *The Information Infrastructure: Reaching Society's Goals*, especially the critical chapters on "Arts, Humanities and Culture on the NII." The final version of the white paper, issued in September 1994, was a major part of the public comment on the Administration's plan and the fullest articulation of the state of humanities computing at that time.

Staff who prepared these papers became keenly aware of how little was known about the range of humanities projects exploiting information technologies and how sorely needed was a research agenda for computing technology focused on the humanities. In future policy discussions, spokesmen for the arts and humanities would need to draw more quickly on facts about the current state of implementation, point to successes, and explain the specialized research needs posed by their fields. To meet these perceived needs, AHIP undertook several projects under the rubric of the Networked Access Project in late 1994 and 1995.

One of these, the Research Agenda Project, was designed to articulate a research agenda for arts and humanities computing and achieve consensus among researchers in technology and the humanities about the critical research needs in this field. Several dozen leaders in the field were asked to identify the important domains in arts and humanities computing research and nominate individuals best situated to summarize the state of research in each. From the nominations, staff selected eight critical areas identified by large numbers of informants and commissioned eight brief papers. In order to allow as many people as possible to have input in shaping the final report, these papers were opened for discussion on the Internet in a private list for a month in early summer of 1995 and for discussion on an open, loosely moderated list in the fall of 1995.

This report, therefore, takes into account ideas from the commissioned papers and the open- and closed-list discussions as well as reviews specifically solicited from other individuals identified during the process. It does not attempt to replace the original papers or discussion, but only to synthesize their most salient aspects and to identify areas for action. The report recognizes that, while resultant research would have a predominantly academic focus, such research would have an impact on the broadest range of practitioners and audiences in the arts and humanities. Its purpose is to offer public policy makers and private foundations the information they need to direct support for arts and humanities computing into areas most critical for the disciplines.

After publication and dissemination of this report to participants in the discussions, AHIP hopes to work with public and private foundations in an effort to increase and coordinate funding in these fields. Future reports on the "State of Networked Cultural Heritage" may be needed to move the agenda forward in future years.

EXECUTIVE SUMMARY

The rapid growth of multimedia computing and the Internet, and the entrance of the commercial sector into information and the education sector previously dominated by academic interests, have raised the stakes for arts and humanities computing. In addition, ongoing reductions in funding for arts, humanities, and educational research (especially from the federal government) have made it imperative that dollars be well spent. In the spring of 1995, the Getty Art History Information Program (AHIP) asked several dozen experts to help it identify the areas of research that they considered critical to future progress in arts and humanities computing and to nominate specialists who could knowledgeably reflect on these domains. Eight individuals were commissioned to write papers on these research issues, and two electronic discussions, open to the Internet community, were conducted to stimulate reaction to their views. This report uses the commissioned papers and discussions as a basis for identifying issues that any research agenda in arts and humanities computing should address.

The papers and discussions exposed four major infrastructural issues and three significant intellectual problems:

◆ *The arts and humanities lack a venue, such as an Annual Review of Arts and Humanities Computing, a conference, or an electronic list, through which progress on the research agenda can be reported and assessed. Support for such research forums is essential.*

◆ *The arts and humanities have not given rise to a field of reflective study, analogous to the history, philosophy, and sociology of science, with a consequent lack of agreement among its practitioners on the fundamental characteristics of the fields and the conditions for successful systems development and evolution. The study of the arts and humanities as fields of human endeavor is necessary to identify the critical success criteria for software and systems.*

◆ *In the vast array of standards-setting and de facto standardization processes under way in the computing industry, the arts and humanities need supported spokespersons to articulate their constituents' requirements. Without such spokespersons, they will have no voice in the development of software, communication and display technologies, and standards governing the range from applications to systems.*

◆ *The arts and humanities need to expose their practitioners, whether academic scholars, museum professionals, or librarians, to the difference that computer-assisted scholarship and teaching could make. Promoting institutional and social changes that are essential to create a hospitable environment for computer-supported arts and humanities is thus a tactical requirement.*

The intellectual issues needing research are considerably more complex:

◆ *Representation — The crucial advantages of digital libraries lie in the flexibility of knowledge representations to support different intellectual perspectives and functionality. However, if they are to create a unified and comprehensive library of useful knowledge, the arts and humanities must make significant progress in the next decade in shared methods of representation.*

◆ *Retrieval — If comprehensive libraries of useful knowledge are created, their use will depend on improved means of access. Discovering appropriate resources in the networked environment and retrieving relevant information in a usable format will be critical. Although the last generation of research in these areas has been far from conclusive, it is clear that distributed networks place new demands on discovery and retrieval.*

◆ *Resource persistence — Even if resources of great utility can be created and found, scholarship will depend on assurance that scholars can cite them at a fixed address, that they will look and behave consistently, and that they will persist over time.*

I. THE PAPERS

When dozens of experts were consulted, in the spring of 1995, about their views of the most important research problems to be resolved for progress to be made in arts and humanities computing, eight topics arose repeatedly as the most significant issues for both the medium- and the long term. Commissioned authors were then asked to identify the nature of the questions raised in each domain, the state of the art, current research of importance, and what future research, if funded, would offer the greatest benefit to the arts and humanities. Seven of the research problem sets can be viewed as occurring in chronological order from the beginning of a scholarly or creative process through to the archival life of its products. The eighth paper addresses societal mechanisms that affect this sequence. Arranged in this order, the eight background papers address:

1. "Tools for Creating and Exploiting Content," by Robert Kolker and Ben Shneiderman, University of Maryland

2. "Knowledge Representation," by Susan Hockey, Center for Electronic Texts in the Humanities, Rutgers and Princeton Universities

3. "Resource Search and Discovery," by Gary Marchionini, University of Maryland

4. "Conversion of Traditional Source Materials into Digital Form," by Anne Kenney, Cornell University

5. "Image and Multimedia Retrieval," by Donna Romer, Eastman Kodak

6. "Learning and Teaching," by Janet Murray, Massachusetts Institute of Technology

7. "Archiving and Authenticity," by David Bearman, Archives & Museum Informatics

8. "New Social and Economic Mechanisms to Encourage Access," by John Garrett, Corporation for National Research Initiatives

This report summarizes some of the points made by both the authors of these background papers and the commentators who participated in the electronic discussions. It builds on an earlier paper in which this author posed questions about the state of activity in important research domains in order to stimulate dialogue as part of the open listserv discussion of these issues on the Internet during October/ November 1995. The online discussions in which this author participated were intentionally open-ended to stimulate debate. The intention of this paper is to bring the discussions to closure, to focus on resolvable issues, and to propose a middle- and long-term agenda for further research. The reader will observe that this discussion does not attempt to fully address each point raised by the contributed papers or by the online discussions; the fault for any resulting imbalance lies entirely with this author.

This report addresses the research papers in the first section, reflecting the judgment of the experts consulted, that these represent the most important research domains. In the second through fourth sections, a series of cross-cutting research questions raised by the commissioned papers and discussions is addressed separately. My intention is not to suggest that the focus of research in arts and humanities computing should be anything other than the topics assigned to the principal authors, but rather to explore the issues they addressed from different intellectual perspectives. I hope this tactic broadens, deepens, and in some cases recontextualizes the points made in the commissioned papers.

A. Tools for Creating and Exploiting Content
Robert Kolker and Ben Shneiderman describe three strands of current research: the Internet, commercially available software, and tools developed for specific research projects or purposes. While Sha Xin Wei of Stanford University correctly suggests that it is more appropriate to see the Internet as infrastructure than as a tool in itself, network-based applications are playing a crucial role in shaping discourse. We know little about how the arts and humanities are being influenced by these tools, or what other network tools might be desirable. Michael Joyce of Vassar College hints at the profundity of such influence by the tools for multimedia authoring and creation of hyper-linked knowledge bases. An unexpected subtext of the Kolker and Shneiderman paper is how much their examples of "successful" electronic support activities involved, and probably depended on, successful human mediation, suggesting a need to train people to use tools rather than basic research into computing capabilities. By implication, continued success would entail funding more demonstration projects in specialized disciplinary applications and ensuring that part of the research plans involve informing other practitioners.

Discussants endorsed the call for research into computer interfaces and interface standards, but it was clear from the discussion that there was disagreement on whether such research was crucial in order to make computers easier for everyone (including humanists) to use, or whether the humanities presented special requirements for interface design. Kolker and Shneiderman stress the need for future research by teams of humanists, specialists in human–computer interaction, and computer scientists to develop interface standards, software tools, and content for specialized arts and humanities users. Most of all they call for support to get tools into the hands of students and faculty. Since this is an infrastructure problem for which upgrading campus-based services is the basic solution, a sound investment would appear to be challenge funding with success measured according to how much the arts and humanities faculty used the installed equipment in teaching and research.

B. Knowledge Representation

The arts and humanities are self-conscious about how they express themselves; indeed, one might reasonably say that the arts and humanities are about the ways in which we express ourselves. Given this fact, it should not surprise us that knowledge representation was discussed by virtually every contributor to the conference and in all the commissioned papers.

The first question, and the fundamental one raised by Susan Hockey in her paper, is what to represent. Not "Which sources should we capture first," but rather, "What about any source do we need to have explicitly represented?" To determine this, research is needed into what we mean by fidelity of representation in order to determine whether fidelity itself is an impossible, or even undesirable, target. Commentators noted that we need representations that are explicit about their limitations, assumptions, and biases; if so, what kinds of annotations are required, and how can they be normalized? The presence of such self-conscious notation was identified as defining the quality of a representation, beyond its mere fidelity to the original. Since most of the research to date has been on text, how can we emphasize all the other modalities that convey artistic and humanistic knowledge? Research into the features of intellectual sources that most fully contribute to interpretation, understanding, and connections would be most useful if those participating either agreed to develop prototype applications or included in their research design steps to bring applications to demonstration.

But even if intellectual perspectives and needs of scholarship can define what is to be represented, we still need to pursue research on how to represent knowledge effectively, and further, how to ensure its future operability. The discussants seemed comfortable with Standard Generalized Markup Language (SGML), but it is clear that extensions, such as HyTime, VRML (Virtual Reality Markup Language), and other representation languages will also need to be employed. Moreover, arts and humanities practitioners will need to better understand why they should not use HTML (Hypertext Markup Language) without guidelines that ensure its conformity with the SGML standard. Standards for representing the content of still images, sounds, motion images, and three-dimensional graphical spaces are still needed. In general, these standards will be beneficial to the arts and humanities if collective agreement is reached on the content of the resource annotations (or "metadata") required for humanistic scholarship. Convening groups to reach consensus on the descriptive elements that best support humanistic research will be productive for many years.

The most vexing issue remains: Why represent knowledge? There is no question that we must by definition represent it for it to be digitally available, or that representations of knowledge are designed to serve specific purposes (or, if not designed for such purposes, are unknowingly valid only for limited purposes), but for what purposes do we want to make knowledge representations? In his comments in the discussion, Michael Buckland of the University of California at Berkeley emphasized the ways in which representations become derived objects in their own right and how semiotics research can be usefully brought to bear on both questions of knowledge representation and questions of what knowledge representations mean in themselves, as material cultural objects. Elsewhere in the discussions the question arose of whether we could, or should, engender a research tradition that asks what meanings digital genres have and for whom and what purposes they exist. We could take the position of technological imperative: that the sources of our civilization's self-knowledge will be "re-presented" digitally and that we must therefore take steps to make the best representations. Or we could try to answer, for different kinds of source genres and media, why certain representations will be better. A research agenda that seeks to answer these questions will, if it produces convincing answers, push the process of digital representation ahead quickly and need not be too costly.

C. Resource Search and Discovery

It is axiomatic that if more and more resources are going to be available electronically and are to be of value to the arts and humanities, we will need to better understand the process by which researchers locate information of interest to them. In what ways is discovery similar to, and how different from, retrieval? We need further research to understand what differentiates and what contributes to the effectiveness of what Gary Marchionini describes as two very different processes. How can the next generation of discovery tools better exploit browsing and take advantage of prior knowledge through guided discovery using authored links and support feedback? How can networked data be standardized so that its "handles" will allow meaningful discovery at a consistent level of detail? What structures and strategies for unique and persistent identification of networked objects will be required, and how can the systems on which electronic objects are created, stored, and accessed ensure such identification? Discovery research is potentially the most important new frontier for information science, and important work can be done at a relatively low cost, because the resources being discovered are publicly available.

Retrieval research, on the other hand, has a long, if checkered, history. What further research on retrieval is needed, and how can past research that addressed central databases be made relevant to the problems of access to distributed resources with different functionalities? How much additional progress can be made in retrieving full text by means of automatic intermediation such as enhanced fuzzy-logic string searching, ranking of results, and using domain-based knowledge with user profiles? How can retrieval be improved by pre-processing with systems tools to index resources automatically, merge thesauri effectively, and analyze resources to support access to them by people with different levels of knowledge or different languages? How can mediated or software-assisted exchanges improve retrieval by enabling us to use knowledge of feedback to increase precision in searches and recall with and beyond browsing? It is not yet clear how much research in artificial intelligence and full-text enhancement is specific to the humanities or how much such research will contribute in the mid-term future, but the long-term promise is great.

Finally, if we are truly to be a multimedia digital culture, what research do we need to enable optical pattern matching, searching for content in oral files, finding relevant chunks of multimedia, locating experiences rather than data, and matching similarities across modalities? Here the humanities are in serious need of approaches and tools that will provide for approximate retrieval: failure to develop such tools means capping the potential of sound and image bases and requiring labor-intensive, single-perspective indexing of the digital source libraries. Investments in automated supports for multimedia indexing and retrieval are crucial, although this research may prove expensive.

D. Conversion of Traditional Source
   Materials into Digital Form

Most knowledge in the arts and humanities is recorded in non-digital formats (most often as printed, typed, or handwritten sources). If, as Anne Kenney contends, we need functionally robust surrogates, and we can decide what kinds of functionality humanists require in their digital representations (as urged under Knowledge Representation), then what methods can we develop (or better yet, what standard methods can we deploy) to acquire that functionality? The research agenda for such capture is as long as the kinds of existing formats in which our knowledge is stored and the kinds of surrogates we need. As methods are suggested and implemented, how can we evaluate them? What methods need to be developed to make conversion cost-effective, and what benefits will lead society to support creation of surrogates that are richer than the originals in their yield of knowledge representation? Only large-scale, technically sophisticated, academically based, multidisciplinary research will push this agenda forward; commercial efforts or individuals are unlikely to contribute much to improving high-quality production processes for digital surrogates.

While it is not, properly speaking, an issue of conversion but of delivery, unless research addresses and resolves questions of how to manage very large collections of digital materials and provide useful access to them, the prospects for large-scale conversion are dim. Research into new compression techniques will be critical in the process. Economics plays a major role, as a business case ultimately must be made for the conversion of content. Moreover, research that leads to evaluation of post-conversion resources will support future conversions and improve methods and technologies of capture and delivery. Support for study of the economics of conversion, and for demonstrating scaleable technologies and organization, will be crucial to the larger vision of an electronically based, internationally accessible, arts and humanities corpus.

Above all, Anne Kenney calls for quality benchmarks (i.e., technical measures that can be applied to digital files), which are crucial if we are to exploit the ongoing development of commercial tools, because only benchmarks will tell us whether our requirements are being, or ever have been, met by off-the-shelf methods. Ultimately, these technologies will be accepted or rejected by the arts and humanities on the basis of display capabilities. But humanists will probably not contribute much to this arena of research, except in the design of user interfaces as discussed earlier by Kolker and Shneiderman.

E. Image and Multimedia Retrieval

Marchionini was not alone in addressing image retrieval; almost everyone bemoaned the state of the art in digital multimedia. Donna Romer made clear in her paper that retrieval results are always based on data representations, but non-textual documents currently defy auto-indexing, and we know little about whether, how, and under what circumstances text-based approaches enable image-based access. Indeed we know little about "likeness" of images, which is the fundamental criterion for retrieval. Constructing an empirical basis for how best to represent sets of images, in addition to or in place of individual images, will also be necessary, since item-level control is often missing in these large image collections. Much of this research will need to begin at the beginning, with documentation of both the resource sets and the user communities. Romer points out that we first need to make sizeable, representative, well-known image sets and establish the characteristics of a variety of "points of view." Such research can be expected to be expensive, time-consuming, and slow to produce results. Nevertheless, accessible multimedia resources are fundamental to the success of a more broadly based arts and humanities.

If we are to create large collections of images for broad-based access, long-term digital image management will require a great deal more technical documentation of the images as objects with a history of capture techniques. Jennifer Trant of AHIP's Imaging Initiative notes that research on image documentation and image quality are issues of crucial concern to the Getty and that these are multidisciplinary endeavors, with implications (and therefore stakeholders) beyond the arts and humanities. The Getty alone cannot sponsor the required research on image quality characteristics and methods of documenting the technical characteristics of digital images (aside from image contents or subjects). Research in this area needs to be accompanied by standardization efforts, education, and implementation strategies, and by proselytizing to other fields. Again, however, such ambitious goals are crucial to making image data usefully available for scholarship and appreciation.

F. Learning and Teaching

Usually it is our lack of understanding of the process of acquiring knowledge, rather than technology, that impedes teaching and learning. But, according to Janet Murray, in some areas simple technological improvements could help in the short term. Because this is one research arena in which progress depends critically on knowing what is known, a major focus of research support should be to inform educators of the state of the research, the state of the tools, and the state of the resources available to them in digital form. Current knowledge in these areas is still quite inadequate, so significant funding is needed to learn more about teaching and learning, test techniques using digital resources, and develop strategies for evaluating teaching and learning as it takes place using digital technologies. These projects are relatively large scale, human intensive, cross-disciplinary, often longitudinal, and will require considerable support over a number of years.

Murray emphasized the need for research in defining curriculum in the light of what the new technologies offer that could not be done previously, and the need for collaborative software development efforts to establish compatible materials and authoring environments customized for the needs of humanists.

G. Archiving and Authenticity

Implicit in David Bearman's assessment of the state of research in archiving is the dramatic shift that has taken place in the past five years as a result of the proliferation of local and wide area networks throughout organizations. These have led to the electronic creation and transmission of virtually all organizational records. While this development affects organizational accountability primarily, the longer-term implications for the arts and humanities are that the record of our culture, as we are creating and recording it today, is increasingly digital. Because software and hardware change so rapidly, all efforts to preserve the original bits on the media on which they were initially stored are doomed. Instead, research must focus on preserving context and meaning, resident in higher-level representations and functionality, while the practical business of managing archival records across time involves copying them onto currently supported devices under the control of newer software. Research into the functional requirements for capturing and maintaining the intellectual character of records as evidence is quite far along, but ongoing support will be needed to standardize approaches, implement solutions, and train arts and humanities professionals (and the organizations in which they work) to archive records of contemporary works in ways that will be usable in the future.

H. New Social and Economic Mechanisms to Encourage Access

Perhaps the most difficult task is to lift ourselves out of our situation and envision different futures. John Garrett was asked not only to do that, but also to identify the research needed to invent those futures and report on the state of knowledge about hypothetical and futuristic social constructs as well as the cultural, intellectual, political, and economic tools needed to construct alternative futures. Neither Garrett, nor the discussion of organizational options and futures, produced a blueprint for social and economic change, but research support directed toward experiments, prototypes, and "re-inventions" is probably the only way that the academic community will move from its current moorings into new waters. While such experiments need not be costly in their infancy, they should be designed to be real players in the real world. Foundations will need to develop tactics that enable them to fund or loan substantial quantities of capital to ensure that start-up ventures representing new ways of organizing the arts and humanities are structured as experiments, not as permanent, resource-creating projects. When such start-up ventures are funded, it is also important to hold at least part of the funding for research into the before and after, and into measurements of individual interactions that support fine-tuning or exploring alternative arrangements.

RESEARCH AGENDA ISSUE:

A theme running consistently through the commissioned papers is that the state of arts and humanities computing is difficult to gauge because it lacks an identity or focus. If the arts and humanities had a venue such as an Annual Review of Arts and Humanities Computing, or if existing mechanisms for reporting on humanities computing issues could be made more responsive to the specific needs of humanities disciplines rather than to technological opportunities, the research agenda could be advanced substantially. A major focus of any concerted research agenda should be to create such a structure.

II. THE NATURE OF THE ARTS AND HUMANITIES

Since the authors were asked to address research issues in humanities and arts computing, it is not surprising that many opened their discussions or prefaced treatment of specific topics by reference to the character of the humanities. Their papers and the online commentaries made clear that further research into how humanists work would help define the functional requirements for supporting their activity. It would be useful not only to define the past, but also to develop baselines that would help us to understand how scholarship is being transformed by computing and digital communications technologies. Serious thought should be given as to how to foster systemic study of the humanities and how to make the results of that research both known and useful to those developing systems to support the arts and humanities.

In the absence of a body of research on the social and intellectual systems of the arts and humanities, authors of the papers and discussants in the electronic conference cited impressionistic and undocumented attributes and derived from them criteria for evaluating the success of computing as a means of supporting these disciplines. Among the characteristics of the humanities the authors identified as important to shaping the research needs of its disciplines were their presumed diversity, complexity of knowledge representation, variability in expression, historicity, textuality, cumulativeness, and genre dependence. Often the authors contrasted these, explicitly or implicitly, with presumed characteristics of the sciences. But in the online discussion, their assumptions about the sciences and social sciences were frequently challenged; although these assertions were also made without reference to a body of research literature that would have supported the debate, such a literature does exist in the history, philosophy, and sociology of science. As Leonard Will of Information Management Consultants in the UK put it, many were "struck by the absence of data on what humanities scholars actually do," despite the self-evident necessity of such research in furthering the agenda of humanities computing. He went on to suggest that research on this aspect of the problem would also begin to resolve the difficult questions of what benefits would be obtained from different kinds of interventions and implementations and by progress in different sub-areas of research.

A. Disciplinary Diversity

One way of thinking about the implications of diversity for formulating the research agenda is to see it as a reflection of material conditions and an impediment to concerted action. Indeed, the way in which it was raised as an issue by Kolker and Shneiderman, who spoke of the "states of the art" within and between disciplines, the disparity of equipment and access (mostly less than ideal) in different institutions, and the absence of humanities researchers among those engaged full-time in humanities-oriented computing research make it appear that diversity is a social and institutional characteristic of the arts and humanities.

However, there may be more fundamental sources of diversity. In online comments, Nora Sabelli of the National Science Foundation and Sha Xin Wei of Stanford University noted that the differences between disciplines might run deeper, reflecting the nature of argument (descriptive, logico-deductive, dialectic) in different fields. They suggested that the humanities might contribute to other fields such as medicine and vice versa, based on diversity among these fundamental dimensions. Sha Xin Wei noted that mathematics was part of the classical humanities curriculum, and that "it consists of intuitions about, and elaboration upon, structures more akin to literature and art than to the empirical sciences."

Such commonalities in intellectual processes should be the link to software functionality, leading to software support for broadly defined styles of reasoning and argumentation, rather than discipline-specific methods.

B. Complexity of Representation

Running through much of the discussion was the contention that the requirements for knowledge representation in the humanities are exceptionally complex. To some extent this opinion reflects the views of specialists for whom off-the-shelf software is inadequate; it may therefore not be specifically about a fundamental characteristic of the humanities, but instead reflect the relative poverty and limited technical investment in humanities computing, which often requires humanists to use tools not specifically created for them. Examples cited, such as multilinguality and methods for treatment of missing data (which is the norm in much humanistic research), are issues in day-to day computing but may not be requirements for a "research" agenda. For example, Janet Murray of MIT, in her comments on the paper by Kolker and Shneiderman, identified two cases in which her work required development of specialized tools to retrieve text from foreign-language video subtitles and support multiple links from any anchor point in an application of a video server. Unfortunately, it is far from clear that these issues of unique software design requirements can be addressed collectively; humanists and their funders may simply have to acknowledge that more funding needs to be directed toward appropriate software for specific tasks at hand.

Susan Hockey referenced a more fundamental aspect of complexity of representation in the humanities, noting the prevalence of a multiplicity of intellectual perspectives which the humanist wants to keep in the picture at all times, since much of the humanities is about styles of discourse and diversity of conceptual frameworks. The requirement to see a textual source simultaneously through a variety of interpretive lenses and to bring them together at various points differs fundamentally from the requirement to see a material object through a variety of optical lenses or wavelengths of light; what humanists mean here, and how computing tools might assist them, deserves further research. The same observation is clearly true of images, although research in this area is much less developed.

C. Variability of Expression

An interesting and important observation made by Gary Marchionini in the context of search and discovery was that the humanities actually encourage differences in ways of expressing ideas for the sake of interesting prose. Not only does this fact defeat many efforts to standardize terminology or provide algorithmic methods of analysis; it poses interesting challenges to intelligent full-text information retrieval. As the concept of "variations on a theme by. . ." makes clear, the concept of derivation as new creation is fundamental to the arts and humanities. Variations become increasingly less derivative and can elaborate ideas far from the original theme, which creates fundamental challenges for developing tools that explore degrees of differences, especially when the original expression is in images and sounds. One of the complicating factors here is that new humanistic works incorporate and elaborate on originals; in the digital environment especially, the act of creativity itself can be blurred.

D. Historical Orientation

Artists and humanists are not alone in dealing with time as a variable in their research, as discussant Warren Sanderson of Concordia University observed, but they are more likely than others to want access to older sources and to need to understand them as they were originally understood. The implications of this orientation for arts and humanities computing research include the following:

◆ Techniques for acquiring digital representations of traditional source materials will continue to be important in the medium term because huge quantities of original materials need to be retrospectively digitized to achieve a critical mass.

◆ Serious research is needed into the fungibility of original sources and into their reusability before great efforts are expended in capturing the material. If certain types of sources are in fact highly fungible, substantial effort could be saved in digitization. If many sources are not reusable, or reusability of sources depends on highly specific technical and intellectual characteristics, wasted investments can be avoided.

◆ Humanists need to develop and employ collective methods for defining representation conventions used in treating source materials, and to incorporate into sources such layered knowledge as commentaries, pathfinders, and attribution tools that both represent a point of view and reflect the understanding of others, from different historical periods, concerning the same objects.

◆ Humanists will be dependent on research that preserves digital signals over long periods of time (as reflected in points made by Peter Graham of Rutgers University) and the meaning of digital representations over time (as stressed by David Bearman of Archives & Museum Informatics).

E. Textual Bias

One of the subtexts of all the discussions was that much of humanities scholarship, outside the arts, has been strongly oriented toward text. Because the authors of the research agenda papers were specifically asked to think about non-textual information, they found many opportunities for additional research presented by image, sound, and multimedia. Contributors to the debate clearly expected that "technology" would solve the problems associated with image standards and with integration of multimedia. In spite of disagreement about whether digital cameras had already achieved resolutions adequate for capturing primary materials, as reflected in exchanges between Kevin Kiernan of the British Library and Anne Kenney of Cornell University, participants expressed no doubt that these pesky technical issues were going to be resolved shortly and without input from the humanities. Therefore, most of the discussion of research implications was focused on the concept of quality as it applies to any representation made for any purpose.

Contributors clearly felt quite comfortable with community-defined standards for knowledge representation, such as the choice of SGML markup and the Document Type Definitions of the Text Encoding Initiative (TEI) for text, but the call for further research began in earnest with markup of image or sound data. As usual, the question of how best to represent the knowledge embedded in such multimedia objects turned on the purpose of representations, the nature of the intended audience, and the meaning of a precision of reference and preservation of context (to use Janet Murray's criteria of quality) when applied to different modalities and different humanities disciplines. It was evident that these questions have not been satisfactorily answered and that substantial research will be required to begin to identify features for integrated multimedia markup and to assess the benefits to artists and humanists of such value-added efforts.

F. Cumulative Character

The arts and humanities are being developed, taught, and thought about on an ongoing basis. For many participants, the design of future teaching and learning was a critical topic of research for humanists. Bob Rosenberg of Rutgers University and Bob Arellano of Brown University urged further examination of the impact of digital delivery systems on learning and organizing teaching resources. Jerrold Maddox of Penn State University expressed concerns that his teaching had by necessity become more exam-based since his students were often 1,000 miles away, and proposed detailed study of the good and bad consequences of distance education. Janet Murray provided examples of how new intellectual paradigms may resonate with the new technologies, as in the teaching of writing. There was no similar discussion of the teaching of art, although oblique reference was made to teaching drama using digital sources of previous performances of the same plays.

What seems most interesting about the discussions of learning and teaching is the role of cumulative knowledge and the representation of cumulative knowledge. Current computing tools provide the best environment we have yet made for exploring such overlays as are created by commentary built up over time. Research into the benefits of using such methods for learning will go a long way toward validating, or discrediting, their use in teaching.

RESEARCH AGENDA ISSUE:

The arts and humanities have not given rise to a field of self-study analogous to the history, philosophy, and sociology of science, long since designated a scholarly discipline in many universities. As a consequence, a lack of agreement on the fundamental characteristics of the fields constituting the arts and humanities precludes the conditions for successful systems development and evolution. A research agenda that does not address how the arts and humanities can become the object of systemic study will have little long-term impact on the state of tools, methodologies, and analytic frameworks for support of these fields.

III. CHALLENGES ACROSS RESEARCH DOMAINS

Several proposed research challenges, while not attributed to the nature of arts and humanities per se, nonetheless applied across disciplines within arts and humanities. These research problems appear to be relevant to any body of organized knowledge elaborated upon by a community of practitioners.

A. Disciplines as Symbolic Systems

Disciplines, including those in the arts and humanities, are formal systems, with languages, representation conventions, and ways of thinking. Moreover, different disciplines evolve different ways of thinking about resources. If we are to develop adequate means for computing to serve "the arts and humanities," understanding the differences between these formal systems is crucial to model our representations of sources correctly. And if we are to decode their representation conventions accurately at a future time, documenting the representation rules we subsequently use will be essential.

Little research has been conducted into the genres of expression used by humanities disciplines and the constantly evolving assumptions underlying them. The claims that humanities disciplines share the need to represent the processes and contexts of creation, and that precision of reference and preservation of context play a special role across disciplines, have as yet little substantiation within the research literature.

The design of the rules for SGML encoding adopted by the TEI, for example, anticipate the ongoing analysis and markup of digitally captured sources. The resulting many-layered representation, carrying perspectives of a number of disciplines and the attributions of many analysts, will make genre analysis a major research issue for humanists. Defining the factors critical to understanding sources specific to different disciplines should inform future guidelines for text representation.

B. Multimedia Representation

To carry modalities of information other than text will require methods for linking one piece of information to another, including objects of different modalities, in ways that reflect the original (pre-digital) intention. Different kinds of objects have different functionality with respect to their links: for example, spoken objects need to be heard, three-dimensional objects need to be moved through and around, and objects that magnify parts of other objects need to be "opened when clicked." At a much more fundamental level, in order to represent multimedia data the way that end users perceive it, humanists need to conduct research into the meanings of the various modalities of information and how meaning is affected when they are combined. A variety of types of information cannot yet be used effectively because we lack ways of representing it digitally that will be available for use by others. To illustrate this point, Susan Hockey identified the problem of representing derived knowledge, while Anne Kenney pointed to pattern matching, object recognition, or raster-to-vector conversion. Thus, subjects for humanities research that would contribute to the evolution of new forms of digital communication include discourse on the construction of "intelligent files" that reflect modes of speaking, have "hot" links, execute scripts, and contain other dynamic and authored elements.

While practical difficulties in managing the evolving new genres such as the corpora and rich webs being created in some disciplines and specialties are not unique to the humanities, humanists have a special role to play in documenting and researching the implications of these new approaches for scholarship and teaching. Several disciplines in the arts and humanities will soon attain the stage at which large enough bodies of digital content exist to constitute the "critical mass" long thought essential for any serious research into the impact of multimedia. Any research agenda needs to join these fields of scholarship in virtual multi-disciplinary laboratories.

C. The Need for Standards

Standards, or the lack of them, were a major concern of most of the authors and are, of course, essential to effective communications. But what was meant by standards, and whether humanities-based research would contribute specially to such standards, was not always clear. Kolker and Shneiderman invoked the need for interface standards and methods of accessing content; their focus on these was supported by commentators who felt that the humanities had special needs for Graphical User Interface (GUI) standards beyond those being met today. They were strongly seconded by Nancy Ide (President, Association of Computers and the Humanities), who viewed the success of electronic means of research and teaching as inevitable but saw the development and pro-mulgation of appropriate user interface standards as a *sine qua non* of that success. In particular, reference was made to tools that would support annotation and attribution, comparison and presentation, and synthesis. Warren Sanderson of Concordia University envisioned the framework as living between sustained narrative and a database, allowing for drafting, dissemination, amplification and modification, and commentary. "It approaches," he said, "the character of a continuing seminar or colloquium." Sha Xin Wei cautioned, however, that standardized environment elements, such as the World Wide Web protocol, are not really tools but simply infrastructure and that toolsets will be constructed around scholarly tasks and disciplines.

Susan Hockey explored the role of meta-data as independent representations of the logical and physical source, which led to the importance of SGML for preventing obsolescence in text representation. She noted humanists' need for multiple parallel hierarchies in SGML (which remains a research problem) and the limitations of HTML in this respect. It is not evident that new standards are required for representing significant intellectual features of texts or multimedia, specific to the humanities; agreement on what meta-data ought to be employed for these purposes calls for further research.

Janet Murray foresaw that teaching from texts will be severely hampered unless we can develop standards for text management software, but these are only the tip of a larger iceberg: application interoperability standards of value to education. Ron Overman of the National Science Foundation added that ethnographic databases, geographical databases, economic history databases, and databased video all represent environments needing common authoring and retrieval tools and standard methods to enhance intra- and interdisciplinary research. Because there is little reason to believe that interoperability standards are more necessary in the humanities than in other areas of endeavor, however, a research focus specific to the arts and humanities seems unnecessary.

In some areas, the arts and humanities could be special beneficiaries. Current standards for digitization of images are confined to technical standards necessary to record pixels, rather than intellectual standards for recording the content and ideas the images represent. While technical standards help ensure quality of capture, Anne Kenney makes it clear that the humanities will always need to ask "quality for what purpose"; content-level standards, based on intended use, will require further research into those uses. Of course, if the images are in color, humanists will be concerned that the surrogate has the same color as the original, a nearly impossible goal without standards for color management and display, which are still in their infancy.

System and architecture standards were not forgotten. John Garrett noted the crucial need for reliable, standard infrastructures. Several such standards would be of special importance to the humanities, including location-independent naming of objects and registration methods for digital objects that will protect intellectual property and ensure credit. David Bearman called for immediate investment in standards for meta-data encapsulation of records to protect their qualities as evidence, to fulfill an essential aspect of trustworthy and reliable testimony critically important to all scholarship.

RESEARCH AGENDA ISSUES:

If the arts and humanities are to be successful in influencing the development of software, display and telecommunications technologies, and standards ranging from applications to systems, they will require supported spokespersons capable of taking their position in the vast array of standards-setting and de facto standardization processes under way in the computing industry. Substantial costs are entailed to retain the technical expertise to play effectively in the standards arena. Further investments will be required to maintain regular contact with arts and humanities scholars and credibly represent their interests. A research agenda that overlooks the need to support such infrastructure will have little impact on the fundamental characteristics of computing and communications technologies.

IV. INSTITUTIONAL CHALLENGES
The task of writing about new societal mechanisms was assigned to John Garrett. A broadly based response urged further study of emerging institutions and imagined institutional arrangements, with experimentation the frequently recommended means of exploring new institutional structures. Virtually every participant highlighted the need to understand and better manage the social dimensions, organizational challenges, and economic constructs that the advent of digital networked communica-

tions had brought to the humanities. The called-for research ranged from providing support and tools for humanistic scholars and developing more cost-effective methods of data capture, conversion, delivery, and distribution to more fundamental issues of promotion and tenure, peer review, access to resources, and support of "trailblazers." While the need for research in these areas is not confined to the humanities, humanists keenly feel the absence of a framework for entering the digital age.

A. Distribution of Scholarly Knowledge
Communication is, above all else, essential to the arts and humanities. The system of dissemination that supports them, in its broadest definition, encompasses all means of publishing and performing. The significant changes that this system is undergoing raise many questions about its direction and method of getting there.

Scholarship requires repositories of knowledge and communities of debate. Building libraries is the first task, and it is evident that we do not know technically how to go about the capture of digital information, where to get the funds, or where to begin. Katherine Jones-Garmil of Harvard University identified the serious need to move beyond the "greatest hits," or works of canonical importance in a given discipline, to the primary sources of real value to scholarship. She and others called both for evolution of the electronic journal and for research into the benefits and drawbacks of electronic-only dissemination of current knowledge.

Accessing the resources, if and when they are digitized, is no easier. Toni Petersen of the Art & Architecture Thesaurus noted that "incredible funding resources are going to have to be applied to improve" discovery and retrieval. Research by the Coalition for Networked Information over the past year has suggested the same. Even when electronic representations have been found, getting them to those who need them is no trivial matter. Kolker and Shneiderman joined Janet Murray in calling for research on how best to deliver electronic resources to students. The Museum Educational Site Licensing Project in the United States, which has drawn attention to this problem, is among the experimental fields in which research on these questions can be pursued.

Once data is delivered, interpreting what has been sent and providing tools for understanding it presents no small task. Anne Kenney and

Janet Murray pointed to the large compendia and discipline-based projects that are creating a new resource, rather than simply a library of old sources, and to the social implications of creating "course length" hypermedia. How, they and others asked, will the role of the scholar, as teacher, as author, as reader, or as curriculum developer change?

Challenging part of the framework suggested by John Garrett, Paul Peters of the Coalition for Networked Information pointed to numerous studies, and to the need for many more, examining how traditional roles in the production and dissemination of scholarship are breaking down and what is replacing them. The systems being studied are essentially those of the traditional scholarly publishing chain, but other ecologies need analysis, too: the authors of fiction, poetry, music, dance, theater, film, and software are part of different dissemination chains that are no less affected by change, perhaps even more so.

B. Education
Despite the great promise of electronically networked resources, higher education has yet to capitalize on them as supports for its research, teaching, or service roles. The concerns of elementary and secondary education were nearly invisible in the online discussion, but surely they will have as great an impact as the universities on the electronically resourced future of learning. In any case, a research agenda that does not look equally seriously at the implications of arts and humanities computing for K-12 education, and for lifelong learning, as it does at higher education will fail in the most important respect: it will lack relevance to the social context in which the case for arts and humanities computing must ultimately be made.

But this aspect of the research agenda is formidable. To begin with, we know very little about the use and impact of digital surrogates in learning. It may be too early to study the effects of new media, and we may still know too little about learning itself. But it is not too early to formulate questions and to begin to gather baseline data from which to assess the inroads made by new methods of teaching and learning based on electronic resources and software-assisted methods. Small-scale, controlled studies, with substantial qualitative aspects, could first serve as the basis for larger, quantitative studies that make comparative assessments.

C. Law
Changes in society lead to changes in law. In the case of electronic resources in arts and humanities, these changes are still too inchoate to provide adequate support for potential developments such as the copyright of electronic resources in education and the reliance on electronic evidence for historical study. Janet Murray, and Jennifer Trant of AHIP's Imaging Initiative, expressed the contemporary uncertainty regarding intellectual property law. Specifically, these uncertainties are seen as having current negative impact on media studies, but the longer-term impacts will be on all uses of historical resources that need to be converted to electronic form. David Bearman pointed to legal uncertainties about what it means to preserve electronic evidence and how failure on the part of governments and individuals to create authoritative electronic records will impede future historical research.

Research, combined with advocacy, can advance arts and humanities interests within legal frameworks. Research that defines specific harms and identifies equally specific remedies is essential to future electronic scholarship. The pace of legislation is generally faster than that of research. Thus the challenge is to fund anticipatory research by policy research groups already in place.

D. Economics
During the conference, there was only indirect discussion of the importance of economic research to the agenda of humanities computing. Yet humanists often feel that the agenda for software research, for example, is being set by commercial firms with needs and priorities different from theirs, and that the nature of the medium and its use is being determined by info-tainment rather than by educational interests. Although considerable research has been conducted on the economics of the current, paper-based information delivery models in libraries, the discussion neither referenced this work nor called for more. Nevertheless, only a better understanding of the economics of the systems that support arts and humanities will change both those systems and the flows of resources through them, to achieve desired new ends. Any serious research agenda for arts and humanities computing will support research on the economics of capture, storage, retrieval, delivery, and use of electronic resources, as well as examine the costs of failure to develop an

appropriate mechanism for arts and humanities to exploit computing capabilities.

E. Communication Technology

The attention given by the authors to issues of communication, collaboration, and dissemination highlighted the transition over the last decade from freestanding to networked computing. Virtually all the authors, while celebrating the virtues of the Internet, bemoaned its primitive organization of resources and access methods. Research into both automatic and human-assisted finding tools for making resources known was seen indisputably as yielding the greatest benefit. Its value would increase in proportion to the continued growth of resources and might exceed the benefits of simply adding new materials.

While authors and discussants pointed to exemplary Internet sites, they acknowledged the severe limitations of common knowledge-representation toolsets such as those based on HTML. The advantages of mixed media in the digital network nevertheless raise a host of research problems, ranging from such basic technical issues as linking objects of different modalities and determining appropriate levels of compression research to more fundamental demands for greater understanding of user needs and perceptions. The sense that digital multimedia is the beginning of a new means of human communication has yet to give birth to a research framework in which the meaning of this revolution, and the means for promoting it, can be understood.

The concern for the instability of the current network was accompanied by a certain despair over how the arts and humanities could influence it to become more the kind of long-term, supportive communications environment they need. Specifically, dramatic improvements in display technologies and interoperability standards need to be developed and sustained to overcome the current impermanence of the virtual networked library. Of critical importance is research to identify methods to prevent destruction of the last or archival copy of a work as well as means to ensure that archiving solutions in a networked environment will prove both scaleable and susceptible to implementation.

Finally, the participants saw a need for new tools. In the face of their inability to digest the thousands of new tools being thrust out into the market annually, there was nevertheless a sense that some classes of tools were not fully understood, would not be made by the commercial sector, or would not be effectively used by arts and humanities scholars without substantial new support. In addition to better methods of search and discovery, the leading requirement was for stronger mechanisms to support editorial or critical review and the analytic and annotation facilities they required. The widespread call for tools that could evaluate, automatically summarize, and integrate different sources raised the implicit question of how the humanist's role will change when software performs these traditional intellectual tasks for the scholar.

The absence of baseline data about what communications and computing facilities the arts and humanities are using, and for what purposes, makes it difficult to identify where best to invest in research. The first research issue, therefore, will be to establish such baselines.

F. People

In the midst of large-scale social change, understanding what is happening to people and their interactions with technology is critical to making it work better. This requires not a one-time study, but rather an ongoing effort of many different disciplines over the foreseeable future. What kinds of questions will have to be asked, again and again, to navigate through this transition? What skills are needed, what meanings are to be imparted, what methods are to be employed?

Kolker and Shneiderman called for ongoing research into the shifting computer-literacy needs of faculty and students. One could reasonably extend this call to the general public and to younger students as well. Probably of equal importance to the humanities, as Anne Kenney and Donna Romer pointed out in their discussion of image representation issues, is understanding the meanings that new informational genres will have for their "readers" (even the concept of "reader" will have to give way to a viewer/participant/contributor), how representations will function as surrogates, and how they will serve purposes beyond surrogacy. We will need to continue to explore the cultural and discursive implications of nonlinearity and multiple intellectual perspectives on a single text, issues raised by Susan Hockey. What will the impact of availability be on the perceived usability of images by the end user, as discussed by Anne Kenney?

Skills and meaning will merge in determining what tools future researchers will need and how they will use them. Ongoing research into the demand for structured-vocabulary searching, full-text searching, and searching through knowledge bases using intelligent agents will help change methods of representing knowledge in digital collections. Ongoing research into image analysis and description, indexing, and annotation, and the use of machine intelligence to locate images through pattern matching and object recognition, as called for by Donna Romer, can have equivalent implications. The ultimate need is for a research basis to determine not only the effect of future intelligent objects on scholarship but what kinds of intelligence they, and the systems that support them, ought to have in order to contribute to scholarship.

If research could bring about Gary Marchionini's vision of search and discovery tools integrated with creation, use, and communication tools, how would that vision change his identified need for electronic analogs of existing genres of finding tools? If research establishes that the arts and humanities address an imprecise audience with many varied intellectual perspectives, as numerous commentators suggested, what requirements will this place on software to provide multiple approaches, layered representations, and well-tested interface methods? If, as Donna Romer asks, we can find ways to meaningfully identify content attributes within images for automatic identification by computers, we will still need to understand visual thinking processes (which, in turn, will evolve rapidly). How much more so the representation of motion and music, in which the state of the art today is so primitive?

We can readily agree with Janet Murray that hypermedia authoring and reference environments are urgently needed, yet have no idea of the impact of these tools on the humanities and the arts. The leitmotif here, as John Garrett reminds us, is that there is a strong interplay among technology, scholarship, and society and that we have yet to begin the job of studying these variables to tune the system. What far-reaching consequences would collaboration tools with mechanisms for assigning responsibility and credit have? How will lowered entry barriers for scholarly publishing affect the humanities?

Finally, Bearman reminds us that the entire concept of evidence has its roots in the culture and that the digital object and digital communications will transform both our concepts of evidence and the literary warrant for records. How records are used, an area that has long been under-studied, will continue to cry out for attention; in a time of changing methods and problems, the answers will be needed more than ever. Katherine Jones-Garmil of Harvard University adds that the electronic journal and electronic dissemination of research upsets existing paradigms of authenticity and authority.

G. Sources

It is, of course, equally important to understand what is happening to the genres of symbolic expression themselves. Virtually every author stressed the significance of research into electronic genres and our understanding them as means of expression. Kolker and Shneiderman raised the question indirectly in reviewing exemplary Internet sites: what makes a "home page" valuable, effective, or even interesting? Susan Hockey asked more explicitly for research into ways of creating a new genre that she believes is essential for scholarship in the humanities: one in which representations of structure and content are independent, multiple perspectives and versions can be interrelated, and nonlinearity can be supported. Anne Kenney asks us to understand not only what different genres are, but also what are their functional requirements for digital representations to enable us to devise automatic capture settings and make decisions about conversion priorities with automated selection and control.

Michael Joyce of Vassar College contributed numerous examples of collaborative work in MOO (Multi-user Dungeon, Object Oriented) space and of collaborative approaches growing out of the "Computers and Composition" movement that have spawned software, journals, conferences, and even new disciplinary associations. In his view the radically new means of expression interact with the complexity of the "feminist, post-modernist and other radical" content of the expression they have engendered. Donna Romer calls on us to conduct research into the formal properties of genres in different modalities and to explore how to create and exploit an entirely new genre, the "visual thesaurus." And, of course, we have the genre of nonlinear writing, for which we need both better tools and a basis for understanding.

When John Garrett calls for research on resource identification systems he in part reflects the need to identify what a unique resource actually is in an age in which the "original" and the "copy" are indistinguishable and expression involves evolutionary versions, borrowing, and references to external entities. Bearman's model of records as transactions will require research on how best to capture metadata defining the record, creating new genres of communicated transactions and new requirements for robust, functional representations.

RESEARCH AGENDA ISSUES:

Identifying institutional and social changes essential for creating a hospitable environment for computer-supported arts and humanities is critical, since neither the human nor capital resources for changing everything are available. Research that begins to identify critical success factors and locate current barriers will help realize the potential of arts and humanities computing.

Cited e-mail contributions to the discussions (other than those in the commissioned papers). In each case, the names and institutional affiliation of discussion contributors are cited in the text.

BOB ARELLANO (BROWN UNIVERSITY), "RE: LEARNING AND TEACHING," OCTOBER 10, 1995

DAVID BEARMAN (ARCHIVES & MUSEUM INFORMATICS), "RE: ARCHIVING," JULY 16, 1995

MICHAEL BUCKLAND (UNIVERSITY OF CALIFORNIA, BERKELEY), "KNOWLEDGE REPRESENTATION," NOVEMBER 28, 1995

PETER GRAHAM (RUTGERS UNIVERSITY LIBRARIES), "ARCHIVING," JULY 10, 1995

___. "RE: RE: ADVANCED ARCHIVING TECHNOLOGIES," JULY 24, 1995

NANCY IDE (ASSOCIATION FOR COMPUTERS AND THE HUMANITIES), "COMMENTS ON TOOLS FOR CREATING AND EXPLOITING CONTENT," NOVEMBER 15, 1995

KATHERINE JONES-GARMIL (HARVARD UNIVERSITY), [NO SUBJECT LINE], NOVEMBER 15, 1995

MICHAEL JOYCE (VASSAR COLLEGE), "COMMENTS ON LEARNING AND TEACHING PAPER," NOVEMBER 14, 1995

ANNE KENNEY (CORNELL UNIVERSITY), "RE: TOOLS, REPRESENTATION, IMAGE" JULY 19, 1995

KEVIN KIERNAN (UNIVERSITY OF KENTUCKY), "CONVERSION," JUNE 25, 1995

___. "TOOLS, REPRESENTATION, IMAGE," JUNE 27, 1995

JERROLD MADDOX (PENNSYLVANIA STATE UNIVERSITY), "LEARNING AND TEACHING," OCTOBER 6, 1995

JANET MURRAY (MIT), "IMAGINING IDEAL ENVIRONMENTS," JUNE 26, 1995

___. "RE: TOOLS, REPRESENTATION, IMAGE," JUNE 28, 1995

___. "RE: ADVANCED ARCHIVING TECHNOLOGIES," JULY 21, 1995

___. "FUNCTIONALITIES FOR HUMANITIES SCHOLARS," JULY 21, 1995

RON OVERMAN (NSF), "RE: TOOLS FOR CREATING AND EXPLOITING CONTENT PAPER," NOVEMBER 6, 1995

PAUL PETERS (CNI), "JOHN GARRETT'S 'NEW SOCIAL AND ECONOMIC MECHANISMS' PAPER," OCTOBER 11, 1995

TONI PETERSEN (GETTY AHIP, AAT), "RE: RESOURCE SEARCH AND DISCOVERY PAPER," OCTOBER 26, 1995

BOB ROSENBERG (RUTGERS UNIVERSITY), "RE: LEARNING AND TEACHING," OCTOBER 9, 1995

NORA SABELLI (NSF), "RE: HOCKEY PAPER," OCTOBER 26, 1995

JERRY SALTZER (MIT), "RE: ADVANCED ARCHIVING TECHNOLOGIES," JULY 12, 1995

WARREN SANDERSON (CONCORDIA UNIVERSITY), "RESOURCE SEARCH AND DISCOVERY," OCTOBER 11, 1995

JENNIFER TRANT (GETTY AHIP), "RE: TOOLS, REPRESENTATION, IMAGE," JULY 19, 1995

LEONARD WILL (CONSULTANT), [NO SUBJECT LINE], NOVEMBER 28, 1995

SHA XIN WEI (STANFORD UNIVERSITY), "TOOLS FOR CREATING AND EXPLOITING CONTENT," OCTOBER 24, 1995

Synopsis of Research Opportunities and Funding Needs

INTELLECTUAL ISSUES

◆ Shared methods of representation serving different perspectives and functionalities in order to create a unified and comprehensive library of useful knowledge

KNOWLEDGE REPRESENTATION

10ff.	Effective representation of knowledge
10	Different degrees of "fidelity" in knowledge representation
10, 17	Meta-data elements required for humanistic research
10	Application of semiotics research to knowledge representations as material cultural objects
10, 13	Functionalities that humanists require of digital representations
12	Preserving context and meaning in higher-level representations of knowledge
17, 19	The meanings of new information genres, their function as surrogates, and how meaning is affected when genres are combined

CONVERSION, TREATMENT, AND DOCUMENTATION OF SOURCES

10	Features of intellectual sources that help interpret, understand, and connect them
14	Simultaneous multiple interpretations of resources
15	Tools to distinguish degrees of difference between original sources and their various derivations
15f.	Consensus on methods of defining and documenting representation conventions for source materials

MULTIMEDIA

10, 18	Standards for representing content of non-textual media
15	Identifying features for marking up integrated multimedia

◆ Discovery and retrieval in a distributed network environment

11, 17	Methods to manage, and provide access to, large collections of digital materials
11	How retrieval resembles, and differs from, discovery
11	The relevance to the networked environment of prior research on centralized databases

TOOLS

11	Discovery tools that better exploit browsing capabilities and prior knowledge
17	Retrieval tools that support annotation and attribution, comparison and presentation, and synthesis
17	Common authoring and retrieval tools to enhance intra- and interdisciplinary research
20	Automatic and human-assisted discovery tools

TEXT AND EDITING

11   Better tools and techniques for full-text retrieval, including pre-processing, linguistic analysis, and artificial intelligence

20   Mechanisms and analytic/annotation facilities to support editorial or critical review

MULTIMEDIA

11   Retrieval models applicable to multimedia, including optical pattern matching, approximate retrieval, and automated indexing

12   The effectiveness of text-based retrieval in image-based resources

12   Criteria for representing image sets, rather than individual images

16   Methods for linking multimedia information objects, to reflect their pre-digital intention

21   Structured-vocabulary searching, image analysis and description, indexing, annotation, and machine intelligence for retrieval

STANDARDS

11   Data standards for uniquely identifying networked objects, to ensure meaningful discovery at a consistent level of detail

9   Interface standards

◆ Persistence of computerized resources over time to ensure future stability of knowledge

ECONOMIC FACTORS

11   Cost-effective methods for digital conversion of resources

11   Demonstrations of scaleable technologies and organization for digital conversion

15   Retrospective digitization of large quantities of original materials, to achieve a "critical mass"

19f.   The economics of capture, storage, retrieval, delivery, and use of electronic resources; costs of failure to exploit computing capabilities

20   Methods to ensure that networked archiving solutions are scaleable and implementable

QUALITY

11   Criteria for evaluating converted resources, to foster further and improved capture and delivery

11   Quality benchmarks for conversion

12   Image quality characteristics and methods of documenting technical characteristics of digital images

18   Standards for meta-data encapsulation of records, to protect their qualities as evidence

METHODS

11   Compression techniques

13   Standardized approaches, implementation, and training in methods of archiving digital records

15   Preservation of digital signals and their meaning

18   Standards for color management and display

18   Location-independent naming of objects; registration methods for digital objects that protect intellectual property and ensure credit

18   Techniques for creation of digital libraries

20   Display technologies and interoperability standards, to overcome current impermanence of virtual libraries

20   Methods to prevent destruction of archival copies

INFRASTRUCTURAL ISSUES

◆ **Publication, conference, or electronic discussion list through which to report and gauge progress on the research agenda**

8, 13   Publication such as Annual Review of Arts and Humanities Computing to report and assess papers on the research agenda

9   Informing practitioners of research results in specialized disciplinary applications

12   How best to inform educators of the state of research, tools, and digital resources

◆ **Consensus among humanists on fundamental characteristics of their fields, and on criteria for developing software and systems**

UNDERSTANDING

9   Knowledge of how network tools are influencing the arts and humanities

10   Investigation of the meanings of digital genres, their audiences, and their purposes

12   Documentation of resource sets and their user communities, to establish the characteristics of varied "points of view"

13 f.   Understanding humanists' working practices, as a basis for defining functional requirements that support their activity

16   Genres of expression used by humanities disciplines and the evolving assumptions that underlie them

20   Baseline data about use of communication and computing facilities and for what purposes

IMPACT ON TRADITIONAL DISCIPLINES

14   Software for specific humanistic disciplines

16   Understanding of sources specific to different disciplines

17   Linking disciplinary "critical masses" into virtual multidisciplinary laboratories

USE

9, 17   Computer interfaces and interface standards

12   Collaborative software development to create customized authoring environments for humanists

18   Content-level standards based on intended use

◆ **Support for advocacy on behalf of the humanities in technical and standards development**

17   Documentation of implications of new technologies for teaching and scholarship

17   Humanists' needs for standards and techniques beyond those already available

17   Need for humanists to define interoperability standards for their disciplines

◆ **Promoting computer-assisted scholarship and teaching in the arts and humanities**

EDUCATIONAL IMPACT

12   Defining curriculum in light of new technological capabilities

16   Impact of digital delivery systems on learning and organization of resources, for design of future teaching and learning

16   The consequences of distance education

16   Examination of benefits of using computing tools in teaching, to validate or discredit their use

17   Development of standards for application interoperability that are of value to education

18   Effective delivery of electronic resources to students

19   K-12 education and lifelong learning

TRAINING AND USE

9f.   Placing computer and network tools in the hands of students and faculty, and training them in their use

10   Upgrading campus-based services

20   Support for classes of tools that humanists understand poorly or use ineffectively, or that would not be produced commercially

20   Shifting computer-literacy needs of faculty and students

SCHOLARLY COMMUNICATION

17   Evolution of new forms of digital communication through discourse and "intelligent files"

18   Evolution of electronic journals; benefits and drawbacks of electronic-only dissemination of knowledge

ADVOCACY AND PLANNING

9   Demonstration projects in discipline-specific applications

12   Education, implementation strategies, and proselytizing for use of digital images

19   Advancement of arts and humanities interests within legal frameworks; anticipatory research by policy research groups

ADDITIONAL AREAS FOR RESEARCH

INSTITUTIONAL AND SOCIAL IMPACT

13   Experiments, prototypes, and "re-inventions" leading to social and economic change in the humanistic academy

18   Emerging institutions, imagined institutional arrangements, and new institutional structures

18   Management of social dimensions, organizational challenges, and economic constructs resulting from networked communications

19   Breakdown and replacement of traditional roles in production and dissemination of scholarship

20   Human-computer interaction

Tools for Creating and Exploiting Content

Robert Kolker and Ben Shneiderman
University of Maryland

STATE OF THE ART

To be true to the spirit of the humanities, we need to talk about states of the art. The humanities are a large umbrella under which many disciplines carry on many varieties of work, almost all of which may be subdivided into smaller components, down to the unique research done by a particular individual. Because humanities research is only occasionally carried on by teams or under the rubric of a collective project, computer-based tools and access to content are currently (with a few exceptions) distributed across many sites and many individual projects.

In most institutions of higher learning, the humanities include performance and artistic production (theater, music, literature, filmmaking; painting, sculpture, photography); critical and theoretical work (art history, literary theory and criticism, film and media theory and criticism, rhetoric, philosophy, linguistics); research (history, literature, art history; music history; film and communications), and language learning. Frequently these areas intersect.

Given this diversity and the fact that much of the work of the humanities has been traditionally intuitive rather than deductive—and based profoundly on the book—acceptance of technology is slow but increasing at a steady rate. On the most fundamental level of equipment, enormous disparities exist. Most researchers and professors in the humanities still use low-powered DOS-based or Mac computers to do word processing and e-mail. Networking is not universal, though many have some kind of Internet hookup. Some are content with this level of access, but may be unaware of more sophisticated possibilities and opportunities to improve their work lives. With increased training and knowledge of such possibilities, they should be able to raise their interest levels and improve their access, which will mean their work will have a greater impact on their intellectual communities, their students, and their publics.

Others in the humanities are actively exploring how technology can advance their research and teaching. A few devote most of their research to creating computer-based tools for their disciplines. Some team projects are developing common access techniques. For individual research projects, however, even the best work is often—perhaps usually—done without careful attention to human interaction factors.

CURRENT RESEARCH AND ITS PROMISE

The majority of current humanities research can be divided into three categories:

- The Internet, which can be subdivided into electronic discussion groups and Web sites.
- Existing software, such as graphics, presentation, database and database front-ends, and multimedia authoring packages used to develop discipline-specific applications.
- Original software developed for specific or general research projects.

Network access is among the most important tools for the humanities and perhaps the first many faculty use when they step beyond word processing. The wide variety of discussion groups, which permit free circulation of ideas, are especially useful in helping colleagues share information. For example, the NEH-supported H-Net—a network of over 57 humanities listservs supervised by the University of Illinois–Chicago and Michigan State University—provides moderated forums in such areas as diverse as women's history, American studies, ethnic immigration, film history, rural and agricultural studies, and comparative literature and computing. Other humanities electronic discussion groups have waxed and waned over the years, probably because they were too general. But most H-Net groups seem to thrive because of focus and careful supervision.

But these and other network-accessed discussion groups suffer from the lack of a unified network interface and an accessible source of information about their very existence and the procedures necessary for signing up. A single university may have many different ways to make a network terminal connection, from a simple telnet client to a more sophisticated or customized user interface developed for a particular department or college. Typically, someone finds out about one discussion group by already being signed up on another. While directories (of listservs, institutions, archives, bibliographies, people, etc.) exist, they are not commonly known. Finding them requires an existing level of knowledge about how to search the Internet. Such haphazardness of access and knowledge is a primitive constraint, keeping information from people who could benefit from it.

The World Wide Web provides what might be called a general, external common interface for those who can access it. The menu functions of Mosaic or Netscape viewers are the same for anyone using the software. The important consideration, therefore, is the design of a specific site, what information it presents, and how it is organized.

The University of Virginia's Institute for Advanced Technology in the Humanities, directed by John Merritt Unsworth, maintains one of the most advanced sites in humanities research. The interface is simply and clearly organized; the content is rich and growing. IATH provides an outlet for the work of University of Virginia scholars, such as the nineteenth-century scholar and textual theorist Jerome McGann, who is constructing an archive of text, manuscript, and images by the poet and artist Dante Gabriel Rossetti. The historian Edward L. Ayers maintains a site in progress on the Civil War, *The Valley of the Shadow*. The experimental video and computer artist David Blair is constructing an elaborate MOO site for his WaxWeb project. IATH also offers computing resources to a roster of fellows from other universities. In collaboration with North Carolina State University, IATH edits and publishes Oxford University Press's *Postmodern Culture*, one of the few scholarly, refereed, online journals in the humanities. IATH, the most clearly focused site for exploiting humanities content, manages, through a fairly simple and consistent use of HTML, to present a diverse set of issues in text editing,

historical research, and film and cultural studies. It makes use of plain text and multimedia tools and depends on a technologically aware cohort of scholars in the field to access and contribute to it.

Electronic Text Centers, because of licensing and copyright restrictions, provide services that are often restricted to one university community. They have limited Internet and Web access that provide reference and lookup services (card catalogs, and texts of the OED, Shakespeare, and other literary works that can be searched). A few present graphical images of manuscripts. Much literature appears on the Internet—novels, poetry, and drama—but few texts are of dependable authenticity. It will be crucial for Electronic Text Centers, perhaps in conjunction with publishers, to create a body of authorized, searchable texts with access mechanisms universally available. Centers such as the Electronic Text Center of University of Virginia's Alderman Library and The Center for Electronic Texts in the Humanities (a joint project of Princeton and Rutgers universities, also associated with the Text Encoding Initiative) are helping to solve the matter of editorially dependable computer-accessible texts by undertaking major initiatives in digitizing manuscripts and creating authoritative texts using SGML.

There are other, scattered networked projects. A recent Web site, established by the University of Chicago and Notre Dame, exhibits manuscripts by Dante. Among the art exhibits now proliferating, the best design remains that of the Web Louvre project by Nicolas Pioch. The Getty Art History Information Program's Museum Educational Site Licensing Project, a multi-university initiative to explore networked access to museum images, should help organize strategies and methods for networked access to images of art objects.

The use of commercial software packages and, in some instances, the creation of original software, to produce information access programs, multimedia projects, and teaching modules in the humanities are being developed and used by many scholars. However, they are often not widely known beyond the developer of the particular discipline. Well-established programs, such as the Max MIDI composition program, use C language in an object-oriented environment to produce composition modules. The Perseus Project from Harvard uses CD-ROM for multimedia research in ancient Greek history and literature. The Academic Software Development Group at Stanford University has developed Media Weaver, a distributed authoring system for hypermedia and media streams both off- and online, which is currently being used for projects as diverse as Chaucer's poetry and the history of Silicon Valley.

Peter Donaldson, Director of MIT's Shakespeare Multimedia Project, has developed a Mac-based interface that matches the Shakespearean text with moving images (from laserdiscs and Quicktime files) drawn from various filmed versions of the plays. The project allows students to compare different readings by different filmmakers and actors in ways that explain not only the text, but the varieties of cinematic interpretation as well. It offers interesting interactive potential by allowing students to grab and arrange still images onto their own notepad windows.

Cinema would seem a natural subject for computer-accessed study. A number of scholars are exploring ways of digitizing moving images and interactively combining them with text. Some are using a computer interface with laserdisc to create analyses of a single film (such as The Rebecca Project, by Lauren Rabinovitz and Greg Easly at Iowa, which analyzes the Hitchcock film from a number of critical and historical perspectives). Others, such as Robert Kolker, one of the authors of this paper, and Stephen Mamber at UCLA, are experimenting with critical essays using moving images published on the Web and multimedia explorations of the basic cinematic vocabulary, using digitized clips and authored in Asymetrix Toolbook.

Language learning and linguistics are fields of major exploration; a number of interactive projects are based on both existing and new software. Asian languages have received special attention in multimedia teaching programs. Ohio State University and the University of Maryland's University College are creating a multimedia version of a standard Japanese textbook in a project funded by the Annenberg–CPB Project.

Linguistics scholars are developing computer-assisted principle-based parsers (which can give structural descriptions of sentences in more than one language). A database of children's spontaneous speech known as CHILDES has been developed at Carnegie-Mellon University with NSF funding.

FUTURE RESEARCH NEEDS

This very brief and selective survey indicates the plurality of tools and content developed in computer-based and computer-assisted humanities research. What it does not reveal are the intense efforts now being made, and yet to be undertaken, to bring this work to students. Many projects are made for student interaction, but interface designs are as diverse as the projects themselves—requiring skills specific to the project—and student access to computer facilities is far from universal. A very few colleges and universities provide every incoming student with a computer. Others have developed computer lab facilities in which students can do their work. Relatively few have interactive computer teaching theaters where faculty and students can learn in an environment that allows close association between human and machine.

The need for access to hardware is coupled with an even greater need for access to training. Major curricular issues are at stake if computer-aided research and pedagogy are to expand. Introductory courses in computation need to be developed for all students outside the usual computer science curriculum. Humanities faculty members need to be trained in graphical environments so that they can enjoy access to existing humanities content and begin to take part in multimedia authoring.

Work is needed on ways to bring the necessary training to humanities scholars that will 1) inform them of how computers can aid their research; 2) make them comfortable with computer-based tools; and 3) identify and then encourage those who wish to do advanced work in creating tools for teaching and research. This effort must be carried on concurrently with research into the kinds of interface design that would be best for most humanities users.

A major barrier to these users is the lack of interface standards and the need for specialized skills to create and access content. As we said earlier, the work of the humanities is a diverse undertaking with multiple points of view and multiple content. It is an area of many specializations, whose practitioners may not have the skills or the time to devote to authoring and programming. Barriers to access of a variety of computer applications need to be lowered. Standards for multimedia authoring and usable interfaces that can be easily modified to accommodate a variety of content would be extremely useful. Sound, image, and video capture must be

simplified and standardized, as should the programs for integrating them. Not all universities
have software development units available to faculty. In the absence of those, all interested faculty should be able to access simple, universal
tools (for example, HTML and the World Wide
Web). Stand-alone applications need to incorporate a similar, even simpler, set of standards.

Such work would ideally combine the talents of
computer scientists, human–computer interaction researchers, and humanities scholars
developing content and tools. Once these tasks
were accomplished, computer technology would
facilitate the needs of the humanities and yet
remain in harmony with the diverse, explorato-
ry nature of work in the humanities.

KNOWLEDGE REPRESENTATION

Susan Hockey, Center for Electronic Texts in the Humanities

Rutgers and Princeton Universities

STATE OF THE ART

The arts and humanities focus on the study of cultural objects. Knowledge in the arts and humanities can consist of cultural objects themselves, information about those cultural objects, interpretive commentary on those objects, and links or relationships between them. The nature of the objects under study is so broad that the knowledge associated with them can be almost anything, and it can be used and reused for almost any purpose. For example, a text can be part of a large collection studied for literary, linguistic, and historical purposes. The same text can also be analyzed in very fine detail, perhaps even for the punctuation within it and for the physical characteristics of the original source.

The representation of knowledge in electronic format can itself take many forms, and it has taken more than forty years of work with electronic resources to begin to understand the potential and the perils of some of these formats. Source material consisting of text, numeric data, images, sound, and video now exists in electronic form. At a fundamental level, all of these are represented in electronic form as bits, but it is the higher levels of representation (the forms into which the information is organized and the access points to those forms) that define how useful that electronic information might be.

Early projects worked mostly with text, and the efforts of these projects show some of the possible pitfalls in choosing how to represent information. These projects attempted to transcribe electronic text by maintaining as accurate a reproduction of the source as possible. Typographic features such as italic type and footnotes were copied faithfully, making an explicit representation in a different medium (electronic form) of a property of the original medium (print). Typographic features aid the reading process the human performs, but they are ambiguous and so are less suitable to aid any processing done by a machine. It took many years to begin to understand some of the differences between representing knowledge that is intended only to be read, and representing knowledge that can be processed electronically in different ways.

Much of our knowledge about objects or information is implicit in some way or another. We know that the text along the top of a page is a running heading because that is where a heading is normally placed. We can deduce the context or scene depicted in a painting because we know, for example, that the figures shown appear in a particular biblical story in that context. When we see a film clip we can recognize the place where the action is happening or detect a foreign accent in one of the speakers. When we browse a dictionary we know that the item in boldface type at the beginning of an entry is the headword. But when we start to manipulate any of these items electronically this lack of specificity becomes apparent and contextual or other information is needed.

The question then arises of what knowledge should be stored to provide this explicit information. In very many information systems, the representation of knowledge is tied up in some way with particular data structures. Early systems stored databases as "flat files" or single tables with one set of rows and columns, which inevitably meant some restructuring of data before it was entered into the computer to avoid repetitions and to deal with anomalies. Historians and archaeologists commonly complained that this led to simplification of the material. Relational databases provide a more sophisticated data model, but can also suffer from some problems. Not all humanities data fits neatly into sets of tables without some loss of information. Furthermore, the relationships between the items of data need to be defined when the database is initially set up, yet many collections of humanities material are put into electronic form in order to do research that will help to establish the relationships between the items in the collection.

In many current systems the representation of knowledge depends on specific software programs. When items or objects are indexed and access to them is only via special-purpose software that can read those indexes, some of the knowledge becomes dependent on the software and is derived through functions of the software. In some cases it is not even possible to extract the information in the format in which it was entered. Moreover, knowledge that has been created for a specific program or type of computer is less likely to last for a long time. Even if it can be converted easily from one program to another, something may be lost during the conversion, or a different theoretical orientation may be imposed on the material.

Meta-data, or knowledge about the knowledge, is another way of making implicit information more explicit. Some communities recognized the importance of meta-data early on: for example, bibliographic and cataloging data is still fundamentally a means of using electronic means to describe material that is mostly not in electronic form at present. In the 1970s the social science data archiving community created a system for describing its datasets, and these codebooks are almost universally accepted as an essential part of a dataset. Initially created in print form, some are now being converted into electronic form. Meta-data for electronic textual material is in a much more rudimentary form at present, and very few electronic texts have what would now be considered adequate information associated with them. Our understanding of the meta-data requirements for images, sound, and video lags even further behind.

CURRENT RESEARCH

Research during the last ten years has concentrated on establishing ways of storing knowledge in electronic form so that it does not become obsolete, so that it can be reused for different purposes, and so that it is separate from any software that will process it. The Standard Generalized Markup Language (SGML) provides a way of representing information that is independent of any particular hardware or software. For text it consists of plain ASCII files that can be transmitted across any platform and network. SGML is object-oriented. It does not say anything about what will happen to those objects when they are processed electronically; it merely says what they are. Thus different processing programs can operate on the same SGML data. An added benefit of using SGML is the ability to defer

making many decisions which might otherwise have to be made at the start of a project, and which are often regretted later.

SGML can be used to describe anything. Although principally text-oriented, it does not have to work only with text. It can be used for the textual information that must accompany images, sound, and video in order for them to be useful. SGML is not itself an encoding scheme; it is a meta-language within which encoding schemes (SGML tag sets) can be defined. The Text Encoding Initiative (TEI), a major international project in humanities computing and the language industries, has created an SGML tag set suitable for many different applications. Using a modular document structure, the TEI can be used to represent many different text types and many different theoretical orientations. It has tags for the structural components of many text types, and also includes tags for analytic and interpretive information as well. It also has a set of tags which provide an electronic text file header that includes meta-data of various kinds. Another humanities-related SGML application is the Finding Aids project at Berkeley.

The acceptance of SGML is now widespread for commercial as well as academic applications. Its focus on content is appealing, especially when it is not possible to define all the likely functions that can be performed on an electronic text at the start of a project. For text it also enables the meta-data to be encoded using the same syntax as the text itself, which is attractive for processing purposes. SGML software is now becoming much more widely available, and the recent announcement by Novell of an SGML Edition of WordPerfect 6.1 should help to put SGML in mainstream computing. However, SGML basically assumes a single hierarchical structure for a document. Most humanities material has multiple parallel hierarchies, or can even be viewed as webs of information. Efforts to represent these in the current version of SGML are clumsy, since almost all SGML software assumes a single tree structure for processing.

The Hypertext Markup Language (HTML) used by the World Wide Web has perhaps done more than anything to raise awareness of structured text. Even if it does not survive, it will leave a large legacy of text marked up in an SGML-like way. The World Wide Web has also enabled many more people to be aware of network-wide resources in different forms and of the possibility of linking or pointing to information stored else-where on the network. However, the current version of HTML does have limitations in the kinds of material that it can represent, and its encoding tags are mostly presentational. Its meta-data capabilities are also weak.

Alternative approaches to representing text focus more on the appearance of a document. This means that the document is easy to read, but the method is less suitable for long-term storage of material that could be used for many different applications.

A multiplicity of so-called "standards" exist at present for storing images, sound, and video. Conversion from one to another is usually possible, perhaps with some loss of information. Some work has been done in the area of meta-data associated with these formats, but in general this consists of moving information from one system to another in such a way that it can be processed (as opposed to merely being viewed or heard). Size is still a constraint for these types of data, and much effort is of necessity being concentrated on compression techniques for storage and transmission rather than on representation of the information itself.

A number of other representational issues are important for arts and humanities material. Non-standard characters appear regularly. There are many different ways of dealing with these, most of which are incompatible with each other or are functions of specific software programs. In some cases the writing system and the language are treated as the same thing, although only rarely do they have a one-to-one relationship. SGML offers some general-purpose solutions, but these do not appear to be very well implemented at present, and barely at all on the World Wide Web. Dates can be in different calendar systems or can be vague forms like "Hellenistic," but they need to be represented in ways that enable them to be put into chronological order. Similar problems arise with weights and measures, where the units can vary from one culture to another. Names and their relationship to individuals who bear them can also be important. The same name, referring to the same person, can be spelled in different ways. There may also be several individuals with the same name in a collection of material, giving rise in some cases to doubt about whether it is the same person or not.

The need to represent missing or incomplete information in some way is now reasonably well accepted. In some cases it may be important to distinguish between information that does not exist in any way and information that can exist but is not known for this particular instance. The level of certainty about information in arts and humanities data can also be critical, and it is useful to give an indication of this. Similarly, it can be helpful to record who is responsible for decisions about uncertain information or other encoding, and their role in making those decisions.

CRITICAL AREAS FOR FURTHER RESEARCH

Much electronic information in use today has been created with the aim of making a surrogate of something that already exists in another format. Many of the functions performed on that information are the same as those that might be performed on the original: reading, viewing, etc. The electronic environment facilitates other types of processing and analysis. Some of these, like statistical analysis of social science data or text retrieval, are fairly well understood. Others have been barely thought of as yet, but future scholars will probably want to subject electronic information being created today to new and different forms of processing. Gaining a better understanding of the full potential of the electronic medium ought to help us create better and more useful representations of material in electronic form.

Electronic information is mutable and dynamic: changes can be made to it at any time. Tracing those changes becomes important for future users, but we do not yet have a universally recognized way of recording these. For text we no longer need to write in a single linear stream, stored on rectangular objects like those on which we have written for centuries. We are already seeing hypertext fiction in which the novel has no obvious beginning, middle, or end. This is still in an experimental stage, but we can envisage hypertext writing of scholarly papers in which differing arguments or interpretations are presented in parallel as hypertext links rather than as a single stream of text. Raising awareness of the potential of the electronic medium may thus also help us to create better representations of information.

Current methods of recording meta-data seem to be concentrating on the properties of the original from which the electronic surrogate is made (for example, indexing terms, traditional catalog records, and the like). Yet the properties of the electronic version can also be important. The TEI header is one of the very few attempts to provide meta-data that records the process of creating the surrogate. It includes information about the transcription of the text, whether spelling has been normalized, and the treatment of potentially ambiguous characters like the period. A similar model might be needed for other types of data. Current methods of recording meta-data also seem to be intended mainly for humans to use, but it is likely that in the future they will be read and acted on just as much by computer programs; further research is needed to establish exactly how this might work and what kinds of interoperability are possible between meta-data systems.

With the World Wide Web, we have a glimpse of the potential of a global network of linked resources, where linking mechanisms are likely to become more and more important. In some ways they are fundamental to much work in the humanities, which is about making connections between items of information and associating some intellectual rationale with those connections. At a more practical level, we need ways of linking transcriptions of text to the digital image of the source at a fine level of granularity, and of linking areas of an image to descriptive information about those areas. In most current systems links are software dependent and can only be created and accessed via that software. HyTime, the SGML application for hypermedia time-based information, provides one method of software-independent linking. The TEI Guidelines incorporate a set of linking mechanisms modeled on those in HyTime. Both of these have been little used so far because of a lack of suitable software. More research needs to be done to determine how effective and how usable they are.

Making a link between two or more items implies that a relationship exists between them. The reason for the link is important, and what is needed is a method of representing that reason as well as a way of saying who created the link. It may be that conflicting reasons exist, in which case all need to be represented without one being privileged all the time. Pointers can be multi-headed, in which case all pointers leading from a single item ought to be documented. Links need to made from a single point or span of information to another single point or span of information.

Representing what can be referred to here as "derived knowledge" is also likely to become more important. Derived knowledge is the result of some processing of electronic information (for example, some form of linguistic analysis, or image processing). It may be that, in the current state of our software, such a processing program is not entirely accurate (for example, a word-class tagger giving about 96 percent accuracy), but the processing may take a long time and yield results worth keeping. Ways must be found to associate this with the original material, which also enables the derived knowledge to be updated and amended both automatically and manually.

For the more immediate future, ways of representing some kinds of source material must be developed further to bring them up to the level that already exists for other types. Current methods of encoding newspapers, papyri, inscriptions, text on vases and other artifacts, early printed books, spoken texts, and historical dictionaries are acknowledged to be primitive at present. Linguistic information will become increasingly important as we look toward better retrieval methodologies, and the multilingual aspects of this are very relevant for the arts and humanities. Another area of direct concern at present is what to do about the large amounts of "legacy" data that is already in electronic form, but represented in a way that is now acknowledged to be deficient. Research is needed to perform more "intelligent" conversions that can begin to handle at least some of the incomplete representation of the original in the electronic source.

Cost factors also need to be examined in more detail. Given the high cost of creating electronic resources, it seems important to represent the information in such a way that it can be used for many different purposes. The scheme ought also to be incremental, thus enabling new knowledge to be added to already existing information. In the arts and humanities, the quality of the information is also extremely important. People are often unwilling to use material that is perceived to be inferior in quality to the original. Electronic texts that have obvious typographical errors have been heavily criticized, as have low-resolution images in which the detail cannot be easily seen. Research is needed to determine what is the minimum level of quality acceptable to most users, what are the circumstances where a very high level is essential, and what are the relative costs associated with this.

RESOURCE SEARCH AND DISCOVERY

Gary Marchionini, University of Maryland[i]

Electronic technology has begun to change what information is available [6] and how that information is located and used. The first of such changes are related to remote access: Instead of traveling to the sources of information, scholars use technology to bring information to them. One important consequence of remote access is the broadening of access to students and other novices who would not or could not bear the time and financial costs to travel to libraries, museums, and research institutes, and who might not know what to look for once they arrived. Second, electronic technology brings new genres of information that provide new challenges for search and discovery (e.g., multimedia, interactive ephemera, etc.). Electronic technology exacerbates the traditional problems humanities scholars have found in documenting and locating non-textual materials. Third, change is due to electronic tools and the strategies that electronic representations made possible. The emphasis here is on tools and strategies for resource search and discovery, although we will continue to see closer integration with tools and strategies for creating, using, and communicating information. Such developments imply that creators who choose to become more closely involved with consumers must take more responsibility for documenting their work and making it accessible.

In archives, libraries, and museums, search and discovery are facilitated by finding aids, catalogs, and guides that organize the information space for information seekers. Similar devices are appearing for electronic resources as well. An ongoing research challenge is to discover appropriate representations for information and new search and discovery tools and strategies that leverage the strengths of computers and telecommunications networks.

Search implies an effort to locate a known object; the information seeker has in mind specific characteristics or properties of the object, which are used to specify and guide search activity. Discovery implies an effort to explore some promising space for underspecified or unknown objects; the information seeker has in mind general characteristics or properties that outline an information space in which perceptual and cognitive powers are leveraged to examine candidate objects (elsewhere [10] I have distinguished search and discovery as analytical and browsing information seeking strategies, respectively). In general, discovery emphasizes the location of the promising space, such as a collection or resource (e.g., [2]). Electronic technology provides new tools for each of these classes of strategies and also blurs the traditional boundaries between them.

STATE OF THE ART

Scholarly search and discovery depend on mappings between conceptual space and physical locations. Classification systems organize information objects, thesauri map these organizations onto word labels, and catalogs provide pointers from labels to physical objects. Traditionally, there have been clear demarcations between n-ary information objects such as indexes and catalogs, and primary information objects such as books and physical artifacts. The Internet includes n-ary and primary information objects, and today's interfaces make little distinction between these representations, effectively blurring these boundaries. Thus, electronic technology influences information seeking by changing both the traditional tools that support search and the strategies used for information seeking. Any attempts to develop cataloging schemes for Internet resources must not only take into account these differences but also address the difficulty of documenting dynamic and ephemeral information objects such as ftp and Web sites. It is certainly too soon and probably wrong to aim at developing collection development policies and a master catalog for the Internet as a whole. Nonetheless, specific digital libraries and resource collections have begun to take advantage of information retrieval and information-seeking research to make information more easily and readily available.

Search

Information retrieval research has yielded several approaches to the problem of matching queries to documents and object surrogates. These approaches have traditionally been applied to specific collections of documents (one set of resources) rather than across many different collections. The most basic advantage of text in electronic form is the ability to do string search—to locate all occurrences of a string of characters in a text or corpus. Although many algorithms support string search, inverted file indexes are used in most large-scale systems to support free-text searching. Building on string search techniques, scholars are able to develop concordances (e.g., the Dead Sea Scrolls) and explore word usage frequencies across authors or works (e.g., Thesaurus Linguae Graecae with Pandora). Although many of these efforts are currently restricted to stand-alone, proprietary collections, some are available through the Internet. There has been little progress in indexing non-textual materials, although scene changes and color patterns have been used to augment video and graphical databases. Most non-textual objects are located through textual descriptions or linear scanning.

Another major development in search is the ability to rank documents according to one of many statistical or probabilistic algorithms that use word or phrase frequency data to match queries with documents and rank results accordingly. Although such activities are computationally intensive, today's computers are able to manage representations of documents as n-dimensional vectors and compute similarity measures for documents and queries in n-dimensional space. These approaches have gained commercial appeal (e.g., Dialog's Target and Lexis/Nexis Freestyle); many Internet resources are now using statistical or probabilistic search engines on their servers (e.g., several WAIS-based services are available; the Library of Congress Thomas system uses the Inquiry search engine). In most cases these approaches provide keyword access (based on all words in the corpus except some small set of common words) rather than subject access (based on a carefully constructed controlled vocabulary used by indexers to describe the content of the object). Although ranked retrieval offers good advantages to novice searchers and a viable alternative to Boolean-based search for experienced searchers, we are a long way from providing all and only relevant information to information seekers who pose word-based queries.[ii]

A third set of approaches to searching leverages the logic of discourse or substantial knowledge bases to contextualize queries or to possibly modify them. For example, the Perseus system [4] includes a morphological analyzer that goes beyond string search to provide variant forms for Greek words. Some linguists aim to develop generic grammars that represent the domain of possible logical statements and parsing routines that map natural language queries and documents onto the grammar. Other researchers have developed schemes for taking advantage of meta-knowledge provided by authors or publishing specialists. For example, the Text Encoding Initiative (see Hockey paper in this collection) promotes the use of SGML coding in scholarly texts so that information seekers can use these codes for locating and analyzing texts. Another line of research aims to develop thesauri (e.g., the *Art & Architecture Thesaurus*) that provide controlled entry points for information seekers as they formulate queries or that are applied automatically to modify or expand queries during the retrieval process. Proficient searchers can certainly use a thesaurus to good advantage, but automatic query expansion based on a thesaurus has not generally yielded improved search results (e.g., [8] and [12]).

A fourth class of research aims to develop filtering systems that automatically route potentially relevant information to scholars. Search depends on specification of the sought object and filtering depends on specification of the user. Libraries have traditionally selectively disseminated information to scholars, devoting human effort to scan information services according to institutional and individual interest profiles. Online services allow users to define interest profiles (usually word based), then alert them when information objects arrive that fit the profile (e.g., document delivery services such as UnCover). Different implementations may use any combination of the search algorithms above. On the Internet, several network news filters adapt as users provide positive and negative feedback, and there are programs of research to develop active agents that roam the network to locate profile-appropriate information and sometimes cooperate with other software agents.[iii]

Finally, some research has attempted to automate traditional reference and question answering services. Early efforts used expert-system technology to automate selected reference services; today's efforts aim to go beyond the simple frequently asked question (FAQ) services to develop multiple tiers of online reference support (e.g., [1]).

Discovery

Browsing has many attractions for scholars: exploration, contextualization, and serendipity support the discovery of new connections between known ideas as well as pertinent new informational resources. In manual environments, browsing has been done in specific collections (e.g., a section of shelves). Electronic technology in general and the Internet in particular has greatly expanded the universe of browsable material by bringing it to the information seeker at the desktop. Because the Internet connects a multitude of collections (on all topics, in various media, and using different organizational schemes), discovery has become complicated by the need to first limit browsing to a set of resources. Developing tools and strategies for identifying resources to browse this wealth is thus a primary research challenge.

One form of guided discovery is exemplified by hypertext systems. Most hypertexts use explicit links denoted by link anchors (buttons, highlighted text) to suggest routes for users to follow. In stand-alone hypertext systems (i.e., specific collections), users can navigate effectively by following explicit links. Many scholars consider such links to be editorial acts; thus aggregations of existing materials woven together with hypertext links represent added-value derivative works at least and original scholarly interpretations at best. The immense popularity of the World Wide Web is based on the ease with which users can follow hypertext links with public-domain and easy-to-use client software often called browsers (e.g., Mosaic, Netscape). Hypermedia systems such as Perseus and Piero press the links further by offering implicit or computed links that are made available as the results of queries entered by the user. Electronic texts that use SGML or other markup codes can also offer on-the-fly link constructions that allow information seekers to follow paths defined by their articulated needs rather than predefined links provided by authors or editors. Other approaches include dependencies based on system state (e.g., Petri nets) and scripts that compute links based on

user behavior. Even after users have limited their discovery to a set of pertinent resources, personal discipline is required to remain within that set (e.g., today's browsers do not dynamically limit links to the sites contained in a preliminary selection of resources).

Discovery depends on both locating candidate objects and recognizing relationship(s) between them and the problem under investigation. The interplay between the perceptual aspects of browsing and the cognitive aspects of reflection and evaluation is best supported by systems that present accurate and well-documented representations (i.e., authors or their agents are explicit about their perspective) for objects and allow users rapid and precise control. Direct manipulation interfaces (see Kolker and Shneiderman paper in this collection) best illustrate such interfaces in computing environments. Developments such as the use of thumbnail images as well as text-based descriptions provide new types of surrogates for information objects and support rapid scanning and browsing. Multiple levels of representation for texts are emerging in networked environments as users move from the entire Internet to a subset (possibly ranked) of resource titles to outlines or tables of contents for specific objects to extracts from the objects, to the full representation of the object, and eventually to related objects.

Integration of Search and Discovery

Because electronic environments are blurring demarcations between search and discovery strategies, several developments suggest research directions. First, one way to improve the results of a search is to use relevance feedback. Given a set of objects retrieved for a query, users may be able to identify which are appropriate to the need and which are not. These judgments are fed back to the system and the original query is either modified or a new query is formulated that combines the original query with the additional information gained through feedback. Relevance feedback illustrates the linkage between search and discovery—a search query serves to identify an intellectual neighborhood for the information to examine (often by browsing), and the results of the examination are used to refine the neighborhood. This process mirrors what information seekers do in manual environments, but the computational tools multiply the number of iterations possible per unit time. Just as rapidly displayed, coordinated still images become moving pictures beyond thresholds of 10 to 15 frames per second, this quantitative increase may lead to qualitative shifts in search and discovery. One possible avenue of development in this regard is hierarchical (cascading) dynamic query systems.

Another development that improves search and discovery on the Internet is the use of indexing programs called spiders or robots that systematically link to Web sites, note whether the site has previously been visited, and record basic metadata about each site (sites may also contribute indexing information voluntarily). These programs have made the Web somewhat searchable without constraining the browsing features of servers or clients.[iv] It is important to note that these services do not really represent a catalog of the Internet but rather a listing of home page words. Additionally, to avoid tying up network resources, spiders do not traverse all links in a site (thus a more substantive image of what the site contains and to what it links is not available). Another system[v] provides full-text retrieval but also allows searches on SGML tags and supports multilingual searching. Another approach is illustrated by the Harvest project,[vi] which separates the indexing gatherers from the indexes themselves (brokers). This allows multiple and customized indexes to be tailored for specific communities.

The most important illustrations of integration are the developments in interactive interfaces that closely couple search, evaluation, and re-formulation. Dynamic queries, fisheye views, semantic maps, and other visualization mechanisms illustrate such integration. The quality of electronic display continues to improve as fonts, backgrounds, color, and resolution continue to offer more accurate representations for paper documents and other information objects (see Kolker and Shneiderman). One project that tightly couples textual information and graphical information is the Piero project [9], where relational database entities are linked to a three-dimensional visual database, allowing users to search and discover textile or visually.

Challenges in the Humanities

Although the research and development trends discussed above are applied in all domains, the humanities offers special challenges for search and discovery. First, the humanities celebrate individuality; information resources take many forms, and scholars often resist the imposition of standards. These effects are most apparent in word-based searching, which is complicated by the opposing concerns of creators who endeavor to find unique and figurative language (whether the language of expression is textual, aural, or visual) and searchers who endeavor to map their needs onto language. Asking authors to use standard language is ludicrous, so it remains for editors, librarians, curators, and other information specialists to create customized indexes and guides to the literature. Furthermore, individuality leads to the creation of many fairly small corpora specific to individual scholars rather than few huge collections created by large communities of scientists (e.g., the databases of the Human Genome Project, Earth Observation System databases). Thus, in the humanities, it is especially critical to create and maintain specialized and multiple indexes.

Second, information resources in the humanities are less sensitive to time than resources in the sciences; although some searching in the humanities may be limited by period, the temporal range is typically wide. Thus, finding aids and interfaces may not be able to easily leverage time constraints. Also, these indexes and guides themselves must evolve as word usage evolves over time.

Third, humanities resources are often multi-lingual. Individual works may use expressions from multiple languages, and resources related to a topic or artist may be available in multiple languages. Since English is a de facto standard for science and technology, most of the discovery tools are specific to English (although statistical retrieval techniques such as latent semantic indexing and n-gram analyses (e.g., [3]) have proved generalizable across multiple languages). Machine translation research that uses an inter-lingual language (e.g., [5]) may also prove useful for indexing multilingual corpuses.

Fourth, data acquisition and digitalization are expensive and time-consuming. Simply adopting a controlled vocabulary such as the AAT is a significant change for cataloging new acquisitions, but the retrospective conversion of local cataloging records is intellectually challenging (and controversial) as well as expensive. Also, digitizing text is challenge enough, but much of the content of the humanities is graphical, aural, and three-dimensional. Capturing and storing images or sound at high resolutions is both time-consuming and open to criticism vis-à-vis interpretiveness. Furthermore, the compression scheme used will determine or limit what surrogates can be made available for browsing.

RESEARCH NEEDS AND DIRECTIONS

The special challenges the humanities offer for search and discovery research and the continued evolution of the Internet suggest several themes for future research and development.

Multiple Approaches

Because humanities scholars typically do not look for answers to well-defined questions but rather elaborate threads of discourse, traditional database techniques will not suffice. Humanities scholars and communities need to create and share thematic indexes specific to their own interests and expertise. The metaphor of self-organizing systems—many minds creating entry points for search and discovery—seems more appropriate both for a worldwide network of information and for the spirit of the humanities than the top-down metaphor of one great mind (or committee) that provides an organizational framework for some master index. Because it is in their personal interest to create such thematic indexes, humanities scholars will do so without funding (funding will speed up this process). There are, however, two crucial needs for research support in this regard.

First, we must learn how to aggregate thematic indexes and forge among them links that are activated according to the ontological perspective of the information seeker (this may be thought of as a kind of intellectual interoperability). Thus, information seekers can specify a school of thought and be given sets of links customized to that perspective. Another user with a different perspective would find a different set of links for the same corpus. Research in thesaurus merging ([7]), scheme merging ([11]), and ontology definition ([13]) may eventually be helpful here.

Second, scholars should be encouraged to create pathfinders: guides to themes or topics that give not only give pointers to information resources but also critical commentary and interpretations about those resources. Since it is likely that we will see the continued development of independent, non-standard collections of information—each a uniquely organized expression celebrating human innovation and creativity—it makes sense that these collections themselves should become subject to study, critique, and interpretation. Thus, the purposeful aggregation and added-value commentary that define pathfinders in the humanities represent a form of scholarship that deserves directed research attention. Commentaries have long been part of

scholarly practice in the humanities, but electronic environments provide new possibilities for creating critical threads through the electronic morass that themselves may include interactive aspects; e.g., using a pathfinder a second time will be different since it will take advantage of knowledge about what you have already examined. How this knowledge is used requires creative and scholarly decisions on the part of the creator of the pathfinder.

Because Internet resources will be available to a broad range of users, from children to seasoned scholars, there must be simple as well as powerful tools for search and discovery. Although these are not mutually exclusive requisites, there is a need for developments of progressively powerful tools as well as tools tuned to specific types of users (see Murray paper in this collection). A related need is for systems that provide multilingual interfaces as well as search and discovery tools that handle multilingual corpuses. Both of these needs have positive implications for the humanities, since they will lead to new classes and groups of users.

Other Needs

Clearly, more materials in the humanities need to be transferred to electronic form (see Kenney paper in this collection). Especially for text-based fields, techniques for automatically categorizing and summarizing text fragments will be necessary if information seekers are to maximize their time and memory resources when examining and scanning candidate texts. It seems prudent to look for ways to combine statistical approaches with knowledge-based approaches. For image-based fields, techniques to extract and match patterns must be combined with whatever word-based information is available (see Romer paper in this collection). Regardless of the medium (text, audio, images), interface mechanisms that allow rapid scanning (e.g., zooming and panning; fast-forward, multiple display panels, etc.) are essential to an integrated search and discovery environment.

Finally, scholars must consider their audiences both during and after the creation of their work. First, during creation, the work can be tailored to make it easier for the audience to find it. On the crass side, this is advertising before art; on the scholarly side, this is tailoring expression to be best understood by one's public. Second, after creation, the scholar can point the work at audiences. This is what publishers currently do, but a networked world allows creators to broadcast or narrowcast as they please. This closer link between creators and consumers depends on the development of tools that support creation, communication, and maintenance of digital work. (We can imagine next iterations of hypertext authoring systems such as Storyspace that automatically generate HTML and browser scripts that monitor usage statistics for automatic (or random) mutations or author version control.) Surely, tools will emerge that allow creators to produce viral works that change depending on use (or alternatively, appear in different forms in different environments). Persistence and stability enable static indexing and locational aids to work in today's libraries. We need research to determine how to document, find, and use new genres of interactive and evolving intellectual products.

REFERENCES

1. Ackerman, M. "Answer Garden: A Tool for Growing Organizational Memory." Ph.D. dissertation, Massachusetts Institute of Technology, 1994.

2. Coalition for Networked Information (in preparation). "Networked Information Discovery and Retrieval" (written by Lynch, Summerhill, and Preston). [May be accessed via ftp.cni.org].

3. Cohen, J.D. "Highlights: Language- and Domain-independent Automatic Indexing Terms for Abstracting." *Journal of the American Society for Information Science* 46, no. 3 (1995): 162-174.

4. Crane, G. *Perseus 1.0: Interactive Sources and Studies on Ancient Greece.* New Haven, CT: Yale University Press, 1992.

5. Dorr, B.J. "The Use of Lexical Semantics in Interlingual Machine Translation." *Machine Translation* 7, no. 3 (1992-93): 135-193.

6. Getty Art History Information Program, American Council of Learned Societies, and Coalition for Networked Information. *Humanities and Arts on the Information Highways: A Profile.* Santa Monica, CA: Getty Art History Information Program, 1994.

7. Hafedh, M. and Rada, R. "Merging Thesauri: Principles and Evaluation." *IEEE Transactions on Pattern Analysis and Machine Intelligence* 10, no. 2 (1988): 204-220.

8. Jones, S.; Gatford, M.; Rugg, G.; Hancock-Beaulieu, M.; Robertson, S.; Secker, J.; and Walker, S. "Interactive Thesaurus Navigation: Intelligence Rules OK?" *Journal of the American Society for Information Science* 46, no. 1 (1995): 52-59.

9. Lavin, M. "Researching Visual Images with Computer Graphics." *Computers and the History of Art* 2, no. 2 (1992): 1-5.

10. Marchionini, G. *Information Seeking in Electronic Environments.* New York: Cambridge University Press, 1995.

11. Nica, A., and Rundensteiner, E. "Uniform Structured Document Handling Using a Constraint-based Object Approach." *Proceedings of Advances in Digital Libraries 1995,* pp. 42-59. New York: Springer-Verlag, 1995. [preliminary version]

12. Voorhees, E. "On Expanding Query Vectors with Lexically Related Words." *Proceedings of the Second Text Retrieval Conference (TREC-2),* pp. 223-231. Washington, DC: National Institute of Standards and Technology, 1994.

13. Wiederhold, G.; Wegner, P.; and Ceri, S. "Toward Megaprogramming." *Communications of the ACM* 35, no. 11 (1992): 89-99.

NOTES

i   The author wishes to thank David Bearman, Gregory Crane, Elli Mylonas, and Michael Neuman for comments on a previous version of this essay.

ii See the Center for Intelligent Information Retrieval Web site. For information on Inquiry see http://ciir.cs.umass.edu/.

iii See the Oard web site for a set of pointers to filtering research; http://www.enee.umd.edu/medlab/filter/.

iv For example, Lycos [http://lycos.cs.cmu.edu/] and Yahoo [http://www.yahoo.com/] services allow simple word searching on several million Web sites; Yahoo provides a simple classification system for limiting searching.

v   OpenText [http://www.opentext.com:8080/omw.html]

vi http://harvest.cs.colorado.edu/

CONVERSION OF TRADITIONAL SOURCE MATERIALS INTO DIGITAL FORM

Anne R. Kenney, Cornell University

STATE OF THE ART

This paper will focus on the conversion into electronic form of traditional source materials, including books, journals, manuscripts, graphic materials, and photographs, which serve as the primary documentation for research in the arts and humanities. Although it acknowledges other means for electronic conversion, this paper will emphasize the use of imaging technology to produce digital surrogates for paper- and film-based sources.

Digital images are "electronic photographs" that can accurately render not only the information contained in original documents, but also their layout and presentation, including typeface, annotations, and illustrations. High fidelity to the source material can be obtained in digital images, which can be displayed on-screen or used to produce paper and film copies, or transmitted over networks to researchers around the world. The main drawback to digital images today is that they are "dumb" files, not data that can be manipulated (for example, searched and indexed).

Efforts to convert materials originally created in print form to machine-readable formats have been ongoing for nearly half a century, but the major thrust for arts and humanities research began in the 1970s when important sources in linguistics, classics, religion, and history were converted to electronic texts. The Thesaurus Linguae Graecae (TLG), begun in 1972, was the first significant American conversion effort, and since then a growing number of institutions have initiated major projects to create computer-processible electronic texts. The Center for Electronic Texts in the Humanities (CETH), established by Rutgers and Princeton in 1991, maintains an inventory of existing electronic texts (available through RLIN, the Research Libraries Information Network) and provides summer seminars on setting up and managing electronic text centers.

Such efforts have not sought to replace source documents but to create electronic transcriptions of texts for quantitative and qualitative analysis. The creation of electronic texts has expanded and matured with the development of standardized approaches and common protocols such as the Text Encoding Initiative (TEI), a collaborative effort to define means for encoding machine-readable text that would make electronic exchange feasible; and the widespread adoption of ISO 8879, Standard Generalized Markup Language (SGML), a standard set of instructions for composing structured machine-readable documents that encodes the function rather than the appearance of elements within a document. Notable current efforts in the use of such encoding may be seen on the World Wide Web, which supports Hypertext Markup Language (HTML) documents, and in the California Heritage Digital Image Access project to develop navigation tools to move from online catalog entries to SGML-encoded finding aids and ultimately to a database of digital images documenting California history.

Beginning in the mid-1980s, efforts to use imaging technology to create digital surrogates began, first at the National Library of Medicine, then the National Archives and Records Administration. Although these pioneering efforts provided significant information on the use of digital imaging, they did not result in sustained efforts for several reasons, primarily because they were difficult to justify economically. By the beginning of this decade, however, several developments converged to promote the use of digital imaging, including the following:

♦ dramatic improvements in personal computer technology, including rapidly declining costs coupled with greatly increased power and storage capacity;

♦ consequently, exponential growth in the use of personal computers;

◆ spread of high-speed, high-bandwidth networks accessible to millions worldwide;

◆ emergence of client/server architecture and network-organizing architectures such as the World Wide Web; and

◆ high-quality, high-production scanning systems.

At approximately the same time, a major national initiative to preserve the intellectual content of brittle books through microfilming, spearheaded by the Commission on Preservation and Access and the National Endowment for the Humanities, opened the door for the acceptance of surrogates or replacements for original sources on a grand scale that in turn stimulated the use of digital imaging technology in library applications.

By the mid-1990s, digital imaging was making inroads into the domain hitherto reserved for textual conversion projects. The technological infrastructure had matured enough to support the creation, storage, transmission, and display of digital images. Although digital image files are much larger than equivalent text files, they became cheaper to produce (approximately $.25/image), whereas a fully corrected encoded-text equivalent could cost ten times that amount. Further, many of the documents consulted by researchers, particularly in the arts and humanities, are graphic (photographs, illustrations, prints, drawings, maps) and currently cannot easily be rendered as encoded files. The process of converting text-based material to alphanumeric files through optical character recognition (OCR) programs begins with the creation of digital images and the two steps—imaging and text programming—could be uncoupled and conducted at separate times. Proponents of imaging argue that the latter step could await user needs and capabilities for sophisticated processing of text or the maturation of OCR programs to render more accurate representations of information, particularly for sources in non-Roman languages, handwritten documents, or those that are unevenly printed or produced with older type fonts. Today, imaging is the most cost-effective means for retrospectively converting arts and humanities source materials to digital form, and represents in effect the lowest common denominator for network distribution.

Nonetheless, user expectations at the terminal are that the full text of important sources for their discipline should be available online, quickly accessible, and fully manipulatable. Researchers who accept and use printed books and journals—or even microfilm—often question the value of a digital image surrogate: "What good is this image if I can't search it with keywords?" This question must be satisfactorily addressed in the next few years if digital imaging technology is to be used effectively in a massive conversion of text-based sources and in the development of distributed digital libraries. Currently the most promising use of digital image technology may lie in the rendering of graphic and photographic materials.

CURRENT RESEARCH AND TRENDS

Two major trends have characterized the most significant arts and humanities projects involving the use of digital image technology over the past five to seven years: the move toward the creation of sizeable databases and their initial, non-networked use; and investigations into issues associated with image capture. Among the former, the most noteworthy example is the digitizing of eleven million pages from the Archivo General de Indias in Seville, Spain, that document the Spanish colonization of the Americas. Begun in 1988 as part of the commemoration of the 500th anniversary of Christopher Columbus' discovery of America, this project has completely revolutionized archival practice in the Archivo and researcher use of primary documents. While the scanning (100 dpi, with 16 levels of gray retained) does not capture all the information contained in the source documents, the objective to provide on-screen use has been successfully met. Almost all use of converted materials in research occurs via computer. This project's most significant accomplishment has been the creation of machine-readable finding aids and catalogs providing access to digitally rendered documents down to the item level. Initial plans are being developed to extend network access to the archives to other Spanish repositories. It is uncertain at this time whether or when international access over the Internet will be made available. Consideration is being given to distributing the most significant portion of the collection via CD-ROM.

Other major conversion projects include those conducted at the Library of Congress (American Memory), the National Agriculture Library (which has embraced a goal of replacing the traditional collection with a digital one), the Naval Research Lab (which is converting its large collection of unclassified documents), the National Library of Medicine (where access to 60,000 images of photographs, art work, and printed texts is provided), and Cornell and Yale universities. Within the past year, multi-institutional digital library initiatives in the arts and humanities have been launched or announced, including those at the Library of Congress (to digitize five million pages of American history sources by the year 2000); the Making of America Project (Cornell, Michigan, and other research institutions) to convert and make network-accessible 10,000 volumes (and ultimately 100,000 volumes) on American history; the UNESCO-sponsored Memory of the World Project; and the recently announced initiative to create a national digital library on American heritage and culture by a federation of thirteen research institutions. The federation will formulate selection guidelines, adopt common standards and best practices for conversion, guarantee universal accessibility across the Internet, facilitate archivability and enduring access, and evaluate use and the effects on libraries and other institutions.

Although a number of digital imaging projects are beginning to evaluate the use of digitized material (including those sponsored by the NSF/ARPA, the Mellon Foundation, and the Getty Art History Information Program/MUSE Educational Media), more rhetoric than substantive information has emerged on the impact on scholarly research of creating digital collections and making them accessible over networks. Preliminary information should be forthcoming in the next two years, but comprehensive data may well await the creation of critical masses of digitized collections that can sustain basic research and the means not only for navigating collections but also using them effectively in an online environment.

The second major research trend is defining image capture guidelines and quality assessment processes in the absence of any official standards governing image quality in digital conversion to digitally rendered documents. Under the direction of Michael Ester, the Getty Art History Information Program pioneered work in examining the relationship between image quality and viewer perception, principally with graphic materials. Cornell and, more recently, the Library of Congress in conjunction with Picture Elements have established quality benchmarks

for the conversion of textual sources that are based on the attributes of the source documents themselves and the effects on image quality of resolution, gray scale, and compression. The two institutions have agreed to collaborate on a joint investigation to extend this work to a broad range of source materials. The Research Libraries Group, in cooperation with the Image Permanence Institute, explored technical issues associated with the digital conversion of photographic materials; the latter will build on this effort through a two-year project to conduct both objective and subjective image quality evaluations, develop quality benchmarks, and suggest technical standards for photographic conversion. In two complementary projects, Cornell and Yale universities will examine the costs, processes, and quality implications for creating both digital images and microfilm. Columbia University recently completed a small-scale project on the quality implications of converting oversize color maps.

The principal investigators of these and other projects have argued for digitizing in a manner to ensure full capture of significant information present in the source documents. Some advocate the creation of an "archival" digital master for preservation purposes to replace rapidly deteriorating original source documents. Others consider the cost benefit of selecting, preparing, and digitizing material *once* at a high enough level of quality to avoid the expense of reconverting at a later date when technological advances require or can effectively utilize a richer digital file. Others suggest that derivatives can be created from the master to meet current user needs, and that the quality of these derivatives is directly affected by the quality of the initial capture. Various digital outputs have different quality requirements: high resolution may be required for printed facsimiles but not for on-screen display and use.

NEAR TERM
It is anticipated that within two years, quality benchmarks for image capture for the range of paper- and film-based research materials— including text, line art, halftone, and continuous tone images—will be well defined for a variety of outputs (paper, film, and then on-screen display). For the most part, these will be designed to be system independent, will involve the creation of sophisticated technical test targets, and will be based increasingly on the attributes and functionality characteristic of the source documents themselves. These efforts

began with determining what was technologically possible; current and near-term efforts are directed at determining what is minimally required to satisfy informational capture needs. At present, the trend is to set image quality requirements at a level sufficient to capture significant informational content for a broad range of source documents at the expense of file size so as to avoid the labor and expense of performing item-by-item review.

Although technical, these benchmarks will also take into consideration the subjective evaluation of curators and the needs of researchers. The Image Permanence Institute plans to incorporate psychometric scaling tests in its evaluation of digitally converted photographs and photographic intermediates. Quality assessments will extend beyond capture requirements to the presentation and timeliness of delivery options.

From an industry perspective, research into image capture has slowed; the current emphasis is in bringing to market scanning systems that will offer a range of moderate- to high-quality capture options, but more importantly, faster throughput, greater flexibility in accommodating a variety of source documents, and better calibration across scanners and peripherals (e.g., printers and display devices). The industry will move to high-production gray-scale/color scanning systems that can meet the performance records of bitonal (black-and-white) scanners.

The most promising scanning devices to appear in the next several years will be planetary and digital cameras, such as those now coming on the market from Minolta and Zeutschel, that can handle bound volumes, three-dimensional objects, fragile material, and oversize documents in a non-damaging fashion and without resorting to the creation of photo-intermediates. Unlike flatbed scanners, digital cameras will enable operators to exercise greater control over resolution, lighting, and color balance. It may be several years before digital cameras compete effectively with photography, however. Increased quality and performance can also be anticipated from film scanners, such as the Sunrise scanner that allows for high resolution and gray-scale capture.

Technically sophisticated software for image quality assessment and calibration, such as ImageXpert™, which incorporates fourteen different tests (e.g., modulation transfer function (MTF), signal-to-noise ratio, gray resolution,

dimensional accuracy, color registration and consistency) will provide operator-independent objective tests of system performance. Until recently, such tests were beyond the capabilities of all outside industry or research labs. Color management systems are also now available to calibrate color data across imaging systems and individual components (scanners, monitors, printers). The Munsell Lab at the Rochester Institute of Technology has conducted extensive research on managing color data through the whole digitization process. Several projects focusing on art reproductions, VASARI and Methodology for Art Reproduction in Color (MARC), are exploring alternatives for achieving true color fidelity.

The next generation of software programs to govern image quality should incorporate smart systems for automatic, on-the-fly applications of appropriate capture processes (resolution, gray scale, filters, etc.) based on an assessment of document attributes and explicit institutional/user profile requirements. Early prototypes for this may be seen in the Xerox XDOD "autosegmentation feature" that detects the presence of halftones, applies descreening and halftone filters to those portions while treating text and line art with separate image enhancement algorithms designed to optimize contrast and detail. Instead of creating separate windows for halftone and textual content, a future approach may be to create layered images, with bitonal capture preserved in one layer, tonal reproduction in another, color saturation in a third.

In the longer term, programs will contain features for automatic image quality verification, designed to check not system performance, but the digital files themselves. These will automatically match quality guidelines to desired outputs: paper, film, and (in the case of on-screen display) the monitor's capability.

User requirements for derivative "access" images, including speed of display, browsing versus detailed examination, and color/tonal fidelity, will also become programmable. An early example of such considerations is seen in "progressive transmission," in which a complete but low-resolution image is transferred quickly; detail is added gradually until full image capture is displayed or the reader halts the transmission. Kodak and Live Pictures, Inc. recently signed an agreement to develop capabilities for transmitting, viewing, and manipulating high-quality images with less computing and networking capabilities than are currently required. The Live Picture technology stores images as a sequence of discrete subimages, making it possible to access only those portions needed for transmission or editing at relatively high speeds, even over regular telephone lines.

Some of the more promising industry research focuses on conversion with functionality, bringing intelligence to digital files. Most attention to date has been given to improving the accuracy and performance of OCR technology that can accommodate a broadening range of languages and text-based representations. Adobe Systems' new Acrobat Capture software incorporates OCR technology with bitmap imaging to create text-searchable files while retaining typefaces, graphics, and the original page layout. The combined text and image information present on an illustrated page, for example, are compressed with the most appropriate compression process and combined into a Portable Document Format (PDF) which is smaller than a compressed digital image. The accuracy rate of conversion can be set so that pages or portions of a page that challenge the software's capabilities can be retained as bitmapped images. According to a recent press release, the military is considering using Acrobat Capture to convert twenty million pages of text.

Perhaps more significantly for future navigation of large image databases of mixed content, attention is being paid to pattern matching and object recognition for non-textual information present in digital images: symbols, spatial dimensions, orientation, and facial features, for example. Excaliber is extending its OCR programming to accommodate face recognition, and Photodex is experimenting with database searching via an iconic interface. Providing computer-processible, eye-readable digital images for graphic materials represents the next logical step along this continuum. Initial work has begun to convert raster images to vector images, a popular process used in Geographical Information Systems (GIS) and in engineering and architectural applications. In vectorization, an image is generated by a set of mathematical equations that describe points and locations within the image. They can be computationally altered to provide image functionality and manipulation. The long-range potential is to replace raster images (captured dot by dot) with vector images, which will result in greater functionality for searching, sorting, and manipula-

tion, and greatly reduce storage requirements. Issues associated with quality, however, must be carefully evaluated in this conversion process.

Research, too, is focusing on more efficient compression processes that preserve fidelity and minimize the introduction of artifacts or noise. Work in the development of fractal and wavelet compression techniques is still under way. In an application for Citibank, Kodak is applying highly efficient, syntactical image compression to store photo-identification as barcodes on the back of credit cards. It is envisioned that these will be read at retail stores, where the physical identification of the customer can be verified. This system of compression, based on building a taxonomy of like attributes (e.g., a library of facial features) may ultimately have broad applications for a wide range of source materials.

FUTURE RESEARCH NEEDS
Research needs in the digital conversion of traditional materials fall into three categories: economic, technical, and evaluative. Generally stated, the technology must become cheaper, better, and faster. Economically viable scanning processes and services are critically needed. Higher scanner throughput must be coupled with high-quality image capture capabilities and automated means to ensure consistency of performance and quality control. Research institutions must work with vendors to jointly develop cost-effective imaging service capabilities of high quality and standardized means for creating/capturing the requisite meta-data for ordering and navigating the digital images themselves. The means for capture and indexing should be non-proprietary in nature and should lend themselves to network distribution and future digital applications, such as OCR, structural linking, and visualization techniques. Definitions for creating an audit trail on conversion decisions must be incorporated into header information for each image.

Processes for selection, conversion, intellectual control, and retrieval must be automated or semi-automated if digital imaging is to become an attractive economic alternative. In the near term attention should be directed to matching circulation records with selection decisions, deriving intellectual control from the digital files themselves, evaluating the utility of fast browsing over textual description, and creating a juried, interactive meta-database that could accommodate user input and differentiated levels of access.

Business cases demonstrating the economic advantages of digital imaging applications to research libraries and cultural institutions must be developed and verified. The case for shared responsibility and enhanced access to distributed sources over the institutional ownership of hard-copy sources must be made firmly and convincingly. The Andrew W. Mellon Foundation is funding a number of digital initiatives designed to provide economic comparisons between traditional library costs and those associated with digital library development.

User needs, perceptions, behaviors, and adaptation to online sources must be studied in detail. Preliminary studies suggest that researcher acceptance of image databases will depend on their convenience, speed of access, and degree of user control. It should be presumed that the development of sizeable image databases rich enough to support in-depth research are necessary—but not sufficient—to facilitate scholarly acceptance of the change from hard copy to online resources. Means for navigating, retrieving, annotating, synthesizing, and presenting information at the desktop must also be devised. These capabilities must be developed in an iterative, user-centered fashion because researchers' needs will change with time and their increasing level of sophistication with using digital technology. Greater human control, requiring less human intervention, will be necessary.

Although navigation, retrieval, and utility issues will be central to this research, dramatic improvements in electronic display must be achieved. Research and development of monitors and other projection devices that make it possible to display documents in their original size with full legibility is essential. Ergonomic issues associated with scholarly research habits (e.g., eyestrain, body positioning) deserve greater exploration. Control and flexibility in terms of display, access time, and functionality must rest with the end user. In addition to improved display, research will be needed to tie image presentation more closely to visual perception rather than technologically consistent approaches.

REFERENCES [i]

1. Conway, Paul, and Weaver, Shari. *The Setup Phase of Project Open Book: A Report to the Commission on Preservation and Access on the Status of an Effort to Convert Microfilm to Digital Imagery.* Washington, DC: Committee on Preservation and Access, June 1994.

2. Elkington, Nancy, ed. *Digital Imaging Technology for Preservation.* An RLG Symposium held March 17 and 18, 1994, Cornell University, Ithaca, New York.

3. Ester, Michael. "Draft White Paper on Digital Imaging in the Arts and the Humanities." Presented at the Getty Art History Information Program Initiative on Electronic Imaging and Information Standards, March 3-4, 1994.

4. ___. "Digital Images in the Context of Visual Collections and Scholarship." *Visual Resources* X (1994): 11-24.

5. ___. "Image Quality and Viewer Perception." *LEONARDO.* Digital Image–Digital Cinema Supplemental Issue (1990): 51-63.

6. Kenney, Anne R. "Digital-to-Microfilm Conversion: An Interim Preservation Solution." *Library Resources and Technical Services* 37, no. 4 (October 1993): 380-402, and 38, no. 1 (January 1994): 87-95.

7. Kenney, Anne R., and Chapman, Stephen. *Digital Resolution Requirement for Replacing Text-Based Material: Methods for Benchmarking Image Quality.* Tutorial. Washington, DC: Commission on Preservation and Access, 1995.

8. Kodak Home Page (http://www.kodak.com).

9. Michelson, Avra, and Rothenberg, Jeff. "Scholarly Communication and Information Technology: Exploring the Impact of Changes in the Research Process on Archives." *American Archivist* 55 (Spring 1992): 236-315.

10. Picture Elements, Inc. *Guidelines for Electronic Preservation of Visual Materials,* Part I. Submitted to the Library of Congress, 1995.

11. Reilly, James. "Technical Choices in Digital Imaging." Presentation at the Society of American Archivists Annual Conference, Indianapolis, Indiana, September 1994.

12. ___. "Digital Imaging for Photographic Collections: Foundations for Technical Standards." NEH grant application.

13. Robinson, Peter. *The Digitization of Primary Textual Sources.* Cambridge: Oxford University, Office for Humanities Communication Publications, no. 4, 1993.

14. Stam, Deirdre C. "Pondering Pixeled Pictures: Research Directions in the Digital Imaging of Art Objects." *Visual Resources* X (1994): 25-39.

15. Willis, Don. *A Hybrid Systems Approach to Preservation of Printed Materials.* Washington, DC: Commission on Preservation and Access, 1992.

NOTES

i In addition to the reference list, the author wishes to acknowledge discussions with imaging scientists and research directors, particularly James Reilly of the Image Permanence Institute, Lou Sharpe of Picture Elements, and Don Williams of Eastman Kodak. References cited have been augmented with industry promotional literature, World Wide Web home pages providing hardware and software product announcements, and forecasts in magazines such as *Imaging, Advanced Imaging,* and *Government Imaging.*

IMAGE AND MULTIMEDIA RETRIEVAL

Donna M. Romer, Eastman Kodak

INTRODUCTION

Designing an effective multimedia retrieval system is a complex challenge, primarily because existing guidelines for text-based systems do not entirely apply to the new technology. Fresh analytical challenges confront the multimedia cataloger, for instance, who to optimize retrieval must conceptually and perceptually deconstruct materials across several cognitive dimensions. But existing cataloging tools have yet to catch up with the fact that multimedia description tasks need greater expressive power. This paper discusses these issues as they relate to arts and humanities collections. Sometimes image databases will be used to illustrate a topic, but the central issues are shared broadly by all multimedia applications.

DIGITAL LIBRARIES

The discussion of image databases in the literature over the last several years bears a striking similarity to the literature describing the development of library automation systems. Beginning with basic inventory management concerns, library systems eventually grew more sophisticated in work flow integration, control functions, and enhanced public access.

Today, most image databases are like library automation systems of the early 1980s (i.e., proprietary, and weak on retrieval for all but the most adept). Through the 1980s library systems eventually grew into Integrated Online Library Systems (IOLS), with isolated components united into more fluid structures of communication. Further, productive research into retrieval technologies brought general-purpose access methods to a diverse set of system users beyond the caretakers of a collection. Image databases have not yet smoothly integrated work flows, nor has research resulted in an integrated, widely usable institutional system.

Many years of work, however, preceded IOLS development, especially in classification, cataloging, and public access methods. If one looks back far enough, the bibliographic record as we know it today can even be traced to the cataloging record attributed to Kallimachos in his tenure at the Library of Alexandria [1]. For the items that an image database will need to classify, catalog, and retrieve, there is no corresponding historical tradition that can be drawn from, which is a limiting factor in the development of multimedia applications.

Essentially, this long tradition of organizing ideas, however imperfect, provided the library automation community with a necessary framework on which system developers could build structures. The same generalized methods have not yet materialized for cataloging images and multimedia objects. Many accounts in both the scholarly literature and the trade press describe an organization's rush to acquire multimedia database software, only to face the most pressing problem of all: how to describe the materials in question to achieve effective retrieval from the system just purchased. As these databases scale upward in size, collection managers soon begin to realize that applying existing descriptive methods may be more likely to bury their assets than to provide the wide retrieval they hoped for.

BACKGROUND CONCERNS AND ISSUES

Retrieval technologies are fundamentally judged by how their search tools perform. For database users, the most memorable part of their interaction with the system is with the algorithms that answer their questions. In reality, the key to success is heavily dependent on the quality of the data preparation environment that supports database design, documentation, and cataloging activities. If one looks carefully at why various multimedia projects fail to yield the expected benefits, one often finds that the data preparation step was not adequately formulated. Cataloging itself rests upon yet another layer, data representation, which refers to the choice of abstraction needed to manipulate data on a computer platform. A brief outline of these three issues follows in order to establish a context for later discussion.

DATA REPRESENTATIONS

Text-based descriptions, the most common form of data representation used by database technologies today, have proved to be very adequate representations for text-based materials. What could be better than using words to describe other words and applying linguistic methods computationally to linguistic structures? But how adequate are text-based methods for non-textual materials? We have been proceeding into the multimedia age assuming that people "read" and understand images in the same way that they "read" and understand documents. Multimedia's appeal to several senses and perceptual modes actually challenges the use of words to describe non-textual modalities. Early adopters of multimedia have been confirming this obvious fact as they commonly report an inability to perform comprehensive searches on their newly implemented multimedia systems.

Part of the problem is that existing methods do not go far enough to describe the aspects that differentiate a particular medium from another. For example, in photographic images, the placement of the camera relative to the central area of interest contributes important visual differentiation for "visual" retrieval purposes. Yet even within systems that incorporate camera angle and distance of the subject from the camera, many irregularities are found across this kind of description. Both the lack of standard naming conventions and uneven visual training among catalogers contribute to the problem.

Several initiatives in the research community are today experimenting with non-textual representations for multimedia content, deriving a new alphabet that multimedia systems will use to represent the content of a digital file. (For example, a simple non-textual representation for color is a hue/saturation histogram for red-green-blue expressed as a string of integers.) From an arts and humanities perspective, a fundamental question remains unanswered. Are the non-textual, or "content-based," technologies arriving at representations that have enough expressive power for the materials that arts and humanities collections hold? Since content-based work promises a form of automatic indexing and new avenues for search interfaces, how will traditional cataloging and search

methods be affected? Most significantly, what happens if several competing non-textual methods arrive in the marketplace? How will our carefully crafted interchange standards support the inevitable variety of content-based representations that will emerge?

CATALOGING METHODS

Cataloging is essentially a process of creating intelligent contextual judgments, with the goal of assembling descriptive access points that can not only group items by their similarities, but also distinguish differences within a collection. Cataloging professionals predominantly use text-based structures as decision support tools to construct descriptions for a database. A well-defined protocol and known economy are in place to support this process today. Preserving this investment is an important consideration when evaluating new technologies.

Multimedia content poses brand-new challenges to this effort, given the additional perceptual modalities introduced, which are not evenly represented in the text-based tool set. Image archive managers know all too well what it is to find an image, then hear the further inquiry: "Do you have any others like this?" While thematic content may be readily accessible using cataloged access points, retrieval by purely visual attributes is completely dependent on the personal "memoria technica" formed by the archivist's experience with his or her collection.

The two most pressing issues for cataloging practices today are:

◆ Can existing text-based structures be supplemented to support multimedia cataloging, based on a sound understanding of human cognitive processing of each unique medium?

◆ Can content-based technologies evolve to work cooperatively with text-based methods?

SEARCH MODELS

Database designers create search models to formally describe the primary retrieval tasks a database must support. For example, the user of an inventory database would expect retrieval by part number to be a natural search criterion. Similarly, the user of a music database may expect retrieval by musical phrase to be a criterion for success. Consistent and psychologically informed search models for multimedia retrieval are neither readily available nor obvious. The search models found in both early products and the research literature appear to be driven by what technology is able to do, rather than how people make perceptual sense of different modalities. Traditionally, database technology has assumed that one stores "answers" completely and entirely in the database. But with multimedia retrieval, a greater portion of the "answer" to a search is located in the recognition power of the person initiating the question. The adage "I will know it when I see it" expresses this phenomenon succinctly.

IMAGE DATABASES AND TEXT-BASED CATALOGING

Most image databases today rely on text-based descriptions for cataloging and search purposes. Whether the choice of a word is derived from free-form thought, or from a structured vocabulary such as the *Art & Architecture Thesaurus* (AAT), the "representation" is searched as a unit of text. The fundamental paradigm employed by most systems is matching the impressions and words of the person cataloging an image with the words and affective intention of the person searching for an image.

For arts and humanities collections, several intelligently composed cataloging tools have been developed to enhance consistent description and access. ICONCLASS, the AAT, and the Library of Congress *Thesaurus for Graphic Materials* (LCTGM) are a few of the formal tools currently available. However, are they adequate for building solid descriptive cataloging for image databases? In a forwarded PhotoCD discussion note [2], the California Historical Society noted that combining several formal vocabulary tools to describe their images has much improved access. While the time and cost to complete a data record is increased significantly by this approach, text-based cataloging can be improved by a more formal coordination among existing tools.

As daunting as the problems of the text-based approach is the different thinking modality associated with visual materials. No longer are the variable combinations of image elements, thematic content, and iconographic denotations the only issues of concern. Other more finely shaded interpretations are also required that are difficult to name, such as the formal compositional rendering techniques the artist uses.

For the most part, text-based descriptions in current image databases try to stay close to the realm of the tangible and the nameable. While

this method may work well for very small collections of images, significant problems occur as the image database begins to scale upward in size. It becomes much more difficult to find "the difference that makes the difference" to ensure successful searching.

A contradictory task faces both users and collection managers. How can the power of visual representation be unlocked using descriptive instruments that are not completely suited to visual differentiation? A single word may name an object, such as a clock, but only the limitless variations of compositional characteristics and genre denotations provide the differentiating factor. The old cliché can truly be reversed: A word (in an image database, at least) can be worth much more than a thousand images!

IMAGE DATABASES AND CONTENT-BASED CATALOGING

Over the last several years a number of researchers in computer science and electrical engineering schools have been working on the solution to the text-based dilemma, focusing on creating descriptions from a digital image file itself, a technique commonly called content-based description. The content-based work most notable for arts and humanities emphasizes the recognition and description of color, texture, shape, spatial location, regions of interest, facial characteristics, and (specifically for motion materials) key frames and scene-change detection.

One goal of content-based work is to provide algorithms that can automatically recognize the important features contained in an image without the need for human intervention in the process. Since cataloging is the most expensive step in multimedia database implementation, the promise of content-based methods has a strong appeal for reducing costs (and, one would hope, increasing indexing consistency).

The current state of content-based technology, while very impressive, has yet to provide the generalized methods needed for wide acceptance in the arts and humanities community. Notable work has been produced by the MIT Media Lab in the content-based work specifically related to face, shape, and texture recognition, collected under the application called PhotoBook [3]. Existing commercial applications, such as IBM's Query By Image Content (QBIC), provide consistent representations. See [4] for a recent article in the popular press. The

QBIC technology operates on color, texture, shape, and feature locality.

The content-based representations produced by these projects all have the unique stamp of the research that produced them. If one were able to look at the algorithms that produced the content-based descriptions, they may share some common thought, but most likely there will be significant differences based on local innovations. While the desire may be for content-based work to settle into a consensus form to enable broad usability, the truth is that this is a highly creative and fluid time period for the content-based research community. A stable set of methods on which to build standards are not likely to emerge in the short term. An arts organization may choose a single and unique content-based scheme for its local collection database. But it will be difficult if not impossible to share that same representation with other organizations using different content-based schemes.

This fact should not deter the arts and humanities community from applying the power of content-based technology; on the contrary, this is an ideal time for application needs to be more clearly understood and communicated to the content-based community in order to ensure that the proper forms of representation are being considered and tested. Content-based technology holds great promise for multimedia retrieval and over time will create representations that provide unique dimensions for retrieval.

It is important to note that content-based technologies strive to create mathematical representations of phenomena derived by a set of rules, although a complete rule set for human visual interpretation has not yet been formulated. (A highly readable discussion of this issue is interwoven in a recent NSF/UC Irvine report [5] for digital video systems.) For example, one may observe a content-based database search for images on the dimension of texture, but among the results on the screen are usually some images that make no visual sense at all. To the content-based system it looked right, but to the human visual system there is a mismatch. (Imagine the challenges that connoisseurship studies would provide to content-based research!)

The reality for this technology is that completely automatic content-based recognition is on a very distant horizon. It is much more likely that the cooperative efforts between text-based and content-based methods will yield the most

interesting and useful results for representing image and motion content for a very long time to come.

BUILDING USER-BASED SEARCH MODELS FOR RETRIEVAL

An area that has received very modest attention in the rush to develop image databases is image database user studies. Other papers in this collection will discuss this issue more thoroughly, but I will touch on two issues specifically related to the cataloging and retrieval process. The first issue is related to understanding the kinds of questions that users pose to existing systems to satisfy an existing work process in which they are engaged. The second issue is related to the visual review process that assists users throughout the selection process, since a search is not really over until something has been selected.

SEARCH QUESTIONS

Before images can be cataloged, whether by text- or content-based methods, it is necessary to establish some guidelines for what is important to describe. At the heart of all good database systems is an understanding of the needs of the people who will use the database.

As an example, the Computer Interchange of Museum Information (CIMI) initiative, Project CHIO (Cultural Heritage Information Online), found that this line of inquiry was fundamental to establishing an information sharing model. An IMAGELIB posting entitled "Looking for Mr. Rococo" [6] provided a rich source of discussion about understanding the pattern of museum patrons' search questions in their own words (not filtered through an intermediary). Their inquiry revealed several "points of view" that required more access points than current cataloging practices originally envisioned.

Inquiry "to understand the ecology of questions" is a valuable way to begin laying the foundation for constructing multi-purpose data records that support different kinds of system users. The broadest possible view is to create a cataloging data record whose contents may be rearranged to suit the requirements of multiple "points of view."

A working example of this issue is the research performed for the Kodak Picture Exchange application for commercial photography [7]. Image search questions (in the words of the originator) were collected from both image owners (photo agencies) and image users (graphic artists, art directors). Five common search patterns that emerged from this inquiry were invaluable in establishing a "layered" framework for describing commercial photographic images. In addition, these search patterns made it possible to construct data records that provide access to two different "points of view": that of editorial and advertising users.

While existing search questions cannot possibly model all the search variations a system may receive, this line of analysis provides the database designer with an excellent starting point. Some examples of the search and review patterns that were observed are:

PATTERN	TO SEARCH FOR
Image Elements	*Contexts, objects, actions, places*
Compositional Qualities	*Artistic techniques, genre, medium*
Subjective Responses	*Mood, emotion, subjective evaluations*
Spatial Relationships	*Proximity, placement of objects to one another*
Intellectual Property	*Usage restrictions and pricing*

The importance of a "points of view" inquiry cannot be stressed enough. The understanding gained in this work makes it possible to make conscious choices about levels of cataloging based on user populations. Further, one can create an economic model to support cataloging activities and evaluate cataloging tools against a performance framework.

A VISUAL THINKING MODEL

Studies in art history and visual/mass communications concern the interpretation of visual materials and their analytical deconstruction, but few have specifically tracked the thought process that supports the image search itself. Searching for images may require different thought processes than searching for text-based materials such as documents or books; if so, then multimedia cataloging will have to reflect this fact.

One study by Romer [7] enumerates several visual thinking processes observed with professional photo editors. In some cases the search and review process needs only a software equiv-

alent; in others, there are implications for the cataloging record itself. As an example, two of the visual strategies found are discussed, together with their cataloging implications:

1. Visual thinking is stimulated by images.
People often start to look for images by using images. They may perform a random or directed search through books, catalogs, files, etc.

Implication: Image databases need to provide a structure, like a visual table of contents, that users can access without specifying words. User interaction becomes much easier if a purely visual activity is provided as an initial welcome to a system or during the inevitable "dry spell" frequently experienced during a search session. Not all images in a database would necessarily be candidates for this browse function. Visually appropriate cataloging methods are needed to tag an image as just such a browsing "candidate."

2. Images already selected provide the basis to continue a search.
Once suitable images have been found that are close to the desired visual match, people will often use selected images to submit a request such as "Get me more like the ones I just found."

Implication: An understanding of image similarity features is needed if the "get more like this" scenario is to have good results. Arriving at a robust set of visual similarities for arts and humanities applications is a major challenge, but in the long term will contribute richly to the search environment. To incorporate visual similarity into a cataloging data record will require a deep understanding of each medium and the cognitive process used for interpretation.

RECOMMENDATIONS FOR RESEARCH OPPORTUNITIES

Points of View Studies
Across arts and humanities collections a wide variety of potential users need to be studied. Among the user types chosen, a quantitative methodology should be established for deriving "points of view" frameworks to guide the cataloging process.

As mentioned earlier, the two most important aspects to encapsulate in these studies are the discovery of patterns in user search questions and the perceptual review methods that are employed while refining a search. Both studies will provide the evidence needed to design practical multimedia databases, as well as drive software-related development for user interfaces.

There are few studies in either of these areas, but most notable is the work of P.G.B. Enser for the Hulton Deutsch picture collection [8]. The CIMI discussion around Project CHIO appears to be the most current, active forum in which several "points of view" studies are already under way. This project also presents an opportunity to assess valuable tools such as the *Categories for the Description of Works of Art* with more user-centered understanding derived from "points of view" studies.

Text-based Resources Reviewed for Structure

Existing text-based resources that support cataloging practices need to be reviewed in terms of how well they satisfy the requirements of multimedia retrieval. Preliminary work is needed to develop a list of multimedia retrieval requirements; based on this work, possible projects might be:

◆ An evaluation of existing resources such as the AAT, LCTGM, etc. to determine how well they perform against a multimedia search model derived from "points of view" studies. Support for this approach is partially found in the work of Soergel [9] related to user studies validating the contents of formal cataloging and access tools.

◆ An evaluation to support restructuring hierarchical resources into semantic networks, i.e., structures that represent knowledge in an interconnected manner. Note that the use of a network structure eliminates many of the limitations surrounding hierarchical and faceted thesauri. With a semantic network it is possible to assign several relationships between terms with differing weights to provide a clear notion of the semantic strength between terms.

A particularly lucid theoretical discussion by Janice Woo [10] contrasts the issues of traditional static organizations of concepts to dynamic relationships based on participatory actions (i.e., hierarchical vs. network structures). Chakravarthy [11] presents an excellent and thorough discussion of a prototype image retrieval system supported by semantic network technology (WordNet).

An area of descriptive depth that is important to image retrieval (especially images with his-

toric value) is the precise definition of image elements and their proximal relationship to one another. (Image elements are the tangible people, objects, actions, places, etc. depicted in an image.) Current cataloging practices do not focus on the mundane level of naming individual objects or actions depicted in an image, focusing instead on the descriptions of thematic content and iconographical attributions. For the broadest possible access, though, there is a need to name individual image elements and their relationships to one another in a standard syntax to support precise searching capability (e.g., a man sitting in a carriage in front of Niagara Falls). A consensus on syntax across arts and humanities cataloging will also drive system vendors to incorporate this level of specificity for search support.

A number of "picture description" languages have been proposed by several disciplines. Hibler [12] has suggested a very practical method.

Media Differentiators

Each distinct multimedia type embodies perceptual qualities that make it a unique vehicle for communication. It is important to investigate, and find a cataloging equivalent, for those unique qualities. For example, a photographic image is greatly influenced by the choice of process used. A daguerreotype is different visually from an ambrotype, even though both kinds of imagery are often housed in latched cases. For modern photography, lens and filter choices create visible differences that contribute to the image experience. Being able to recognize and catalog the differences helps an image database support a visually based "get more like this" scenario. A host of other differentiators for image, music, motion, graphics, etc. need further study and articulation.

An example of an excellent manual that presents clear descriptions of visual differentiators for identifying historic photographic processes is Reilly [13].

Visual Thesaurus

Various researchers have created a number of "wish lists" pointing to an idea called variously a visual thesaurus, or picture thesaurus, or picture dictionary. All thinkers have a similar vision: having an image point to its visual "synonym." More complex versions provide a genera–species "divide and conquer" strategy. In all cases, the visual thesaurus provides the structure for placing visually similar things with their relatives. A visual "sense" pervades the similarities across a number of different qualities: genre, compositional technique, time, etc. A recent and excellent example of work in this area is by Lohse [14]. Chang [15] has presented prototypes related to this topic that support visual reasoning using a data structure called VisualNet.

Representative Sets of Images

One obstacle to advancement in content-based technology is the lack of sizeable and realistic data sets tied to application requirements for development and test purposes. It would be immensely valuable to establish a formal method to provide good data sets and share research results broadly between the content-based and arts and humanities communities. (Note that the data sets in use today are typically from clip art CDs that contain very simplistic depictions for analysis.) While some engineering schools work closely with their institutions' art history departments, there is no umbrella organization that then helps to synthesize and interpret implications more broadly.

Music and Motion Representation

In both the library and content-based communities still images have received the greatest attention in the research literature related to representation and cataloging issues. While music and motion imaging are also topics for research, fewer studies exist than for the world of still-image applications. Both music and motion cataloging require more fundamental thought in order to arrive at the right conceptual framework for subsequent implementation.

In music, an early dissertation by Page [16] focused on issues related to the written musical score as the fundamental starting point for musical representation. A paper by Wiggins [17] provides a framework for describing and evaluating music representation systems in a broader context. Hawley [18] analyzes the creation of "structure out of sound" for multimedia retrieval.

Davis [19] presents a motion annotation system in a prototype environment called MediaStreams, which uses icons to describe video content. Csinger [20] proposes a knowledge-based framework to support the human effort required for annotating motion.

CONCLUSION

In summary, image and multimedia databases are heavily dependent on the quality of their stored descriptions, which (whether text- or content-based) provide the foundation for all meaningful interactions with a system. Several descriptive challenges remain to be solved in order to create effective representations. The solutions, as indicated above, appear primarily interdisciplinary. The ideal team would naturally be composed of professionals in information science, electrical engineering/computer science, visual/mass communications, and cognitive psychology. Each of these disciplines holds a portion of the knowledge required to support research in this vital and growing area.

Multimedia "objects" (image, motion, audio, graphics, compound document, etc.) acquire useful descriptive data throughout many different stages of their existence. Some data is acquired automatically by capture devices (such as scanners, or digital cameras), some is added by human intervention through traditional cataloging methods, and yet other data is acquired by automatic, content-based techniques. All these streams of data will require intelligent coordination and constant attention. The end result is to create a richer set of descriptions for retrieval purposes, which can be employed in combination to provide more meaningful access to the vast heritage of the arts and humanities.

REFERENCES

1. Blum, Rudolf. *Kallimachos, The Alexandrian Library and the Origins of Bibliography.* Madison: University of Wisconsin Press, 1991.

2. Elaine Engst (Cornell University), "Cataloging Photographs," 1994. Original sender: Robert MacKimmie (California Historical Society). [Available by e-mail: photo-cd@info.kodak.com].

3. Pentland, A.; Picard, R. W.; Sclaroff, S. *Photobook: Content-Based Manipulation of Image Databases.* MIT Media Laboratory Perceptual Computing Technical Report No. 255. November 1993.

4. Okon, Chris. "IBM's Image Recognition Technology for Databases at Work: QBIC or Not QBIC?" *Advanced Imaging* 10 (May 1995): 63-65.

5. Sklansky, Jack, et al. *Final Report: International Workshop in Digital Video for Intelligent Systems.* December 1993.

6. CIMI List Owner, "Points of View Meeting: Looking for Mr. Rococo," February 13, 1995. [By e-mail: cimil-@lyra.stanford.edu].

7. Romer, Donna M. *A Keyword is Worth 1,000 Images.* Kodak Internal Technical Report. Rochester, NY: Eastman Kodak Company, June 26, 1993.

8. Enser, P.G.B. "Query Analysis in a Visual Information Retrieval Context." *Journal of Documentation & Text Management* 1, no. 1 (1993): 25-52.

9. Soergel, Dagobert. "The Art and Architecture Thesaurus (AAT): A Critical Appraisal." *Visual Resources* X, no. 4 (1995): 369-400.

10. Woo, Janice. "Indexing: At Play in the Fields of Postmodernism." *Visual Resources* X, no. 3 (1994): 283-293.

11. Chakravarthy, Anil Srinivasa. "Information Access and Retrieval with Semantic Background Knowledge." Ph.D. dissertation, Program in Media Arts and Sciences, School of Architecture and Planning, Massachusetts Institute of Technology, June 1995.

12. Hibler, J.N. David; Leung, Clement H.C.; Mannock, Keith L.; and Mwara, Njagi K. "A System for Content-based Storage and Retrieval in an Image Database." SPIE Image Storage and Retrieval Systems 1162 (1992): 80-92.

13. Reilly, James. *Care and Identification of 19th Century Photographic Prints.* Kodak Publication No. G-2S. Rochester, NY: Eastman Kodak Company, 1986.

14. Lohse, Gerald L.; Biolsi, Kevin; Walker, Neff; and Ruetter, Henry H. "A Classification of Visual Representations." *Communications of the ACM* 37, no. 12 (December 1994): 36-49.

15. Chang, Shi-Kuo. "A Visual Language Compiler for Information Retrieval by Visual Reasoning." *IEEE Transactions on Software Engineering* 16, no.10 (October 1990): 1136-1149.

16. Page, Stephen Dowland. "Computer Tools for Music Information Retrieval." Ph.D. dissertation, New College and Programming Research Group, University of Oxford, 1988.

17. Wiggins, Geraint; Miranda, Eduardo; Smaill, Alan; and Harris, Mitch. "A Framework for the Evaluation of Music Representation Systems." *Computer Music Journal* 17, no. 3 (Fall 1993): 31-42.

18. Hawley, M. J. "Structure Out of Sound." Ph.D. dissertation, Media Laboratory, Massachusetts Institute of Technology, 1993.

19. Davis, M.E. "Media Streams: An Iconic Language for Video Annotation." *Proceedings of the IEEE Workshop on Visual Languages, Bergen, Norway,* 1993.

20. Csinger, Andrew, and Booth, Kellogg S. "Reasoning about Video: Knowledge-based Transcription and Presentation." *Proceedings of the 27th Annual Hawaii International Conference on System Sciences,* Hawaii, 1994: 599-608.

Learning and Teaching

Janet H. Murray, Massachusetts Institute of Technology

With the wide availability and increasing usefulness of electronic media, arts and humanities education is poised for significant change. Some of these changes are already under way, others are just beginning to appear on the horizon. They are being met with enthusiasm from some and strong resistance from others. The key to the changes now under way is that a new medium makes possible new methods of teaching and learning and a new epistemology: new structures for representing knowledge. Those who have already been engaged in pushing the boundaries of their disciplines are the most likely to be early adopters of the technology.

RESEARCH AND PRACTICE TO DATE

Writing and Foreign Language Learning

The skill-based disciplines of writing and language learning have been the most active early users of the technology. It is significant, and perhaps forms a useful paradigm for other humanistic disciplines, that in both these cases the adoption was driven by methodological changes.

In the teaching of writing the process model, advocated by theorist-practitioners like Donald Murray, Peter Elbow, and Linda Flowers, was coming into wide acceptance during the late 1970s and early 1980s. The arrival of personal computers starting in the mid-1980s made process teaching much easier by making it easier to create and critique multiple drafts and share the product with peers as well as teachers. Many aids to writing have been created and are in use across the country, most notably The Writer's Workbench (Bell Labs/Colorado State), which includes process aids in addition to its original set of more controversial style checkers, and Daedalus (University of Texas), which allows students to hand in papers online. University-specific networked systems are in use at Carnegie-Mellon, where much imaginative early work was done in modeling a process-approach electronic writing environment, and at MIT, where the system includes an electronic classroom, a facility for adding teacher's corrections to papers handed in electronically, and an online textbook for technical writing. The use of electronic classrooms in which work can be displayed, critiqued, and edited on large-screen displays has made it possible to demonstrate the process of writing in the classroom with an ease not available under the constraints of paper and blackboards. Currently, there is much interest in exploring computers for teaching collaborative writing.

Commercial systems have superseded much of the work on writing software attempted by university-developed systems. Spell-checkers, outliners, annotation icons, and multiple versioning software are all available in word processors or document systems. But the ready availability of commercial products that do the job is the exception, not the rule, for humanities software, and even when commercial products are available their use is often limited by platform dependencies.

Writing shares with foreign language teaching a laboratory approach, and writing centers and language laboratories are natural sites for the adoption of new technology. In foreign languages the interest began even before the advent of the microcomputer. The University of Illinois offered programmed language learning on the mainframe-based PLATO system. The first use of microcomputers was electronic drill programs that relieved the drudgery of workbook grading. Several of these have been developed and are in wide use, including Dasher (University of Iowa), CALLIS (Duke), and MacLang (Harvard). Brigham Young University developed a system for testing students online in order to determine what level of language course to offer them. A more flexible approach was the inclusion of grammar and dictionary information in specialized word processing software, a tactic that was also well used by James Noblitt (University of North Carolina) for foreign language learning. Although some have used the opportunity of computer-based language learning to study the patterns of second-language acquisition, this remains an underdeveloped area of inquiry.

Starting in the early 1980s as the communicative approach to language learning was becoming accepted, multimedia was identified as offering tremendous potential for communicative methodologies. Like the process approach current in writing studies, the communicative approach was a good fit to the medium because it emphasized process over product, stressing the importance of exposure to authentic native speech (which can be delivered on video, richly annotated and cross-referenced), and valuing the acquisition of context-sensitive language functions (such as expressing agreement, asking for help, greeting a friend or a stranger) over the memorization of word lists and grammar paradigms.

Multimedia for language learning was pursued actively at MIT, which produced narratives and documentaries specifically scripted and shot for interactivity (Athena Language Learning Project) and at the University of Iowa (PICT) and the University of Pennsylvania, both of which produced systems for adding subtitling and phrase-by-phrase control to existing visual material. The Iowa project focused on acquiring the rights to foreign television; the Pennsylvania project focused on films available on videodisc. The military service academies have made wide use of interactive video workstations, mostly using re-purposed educational videos, and the CIA is currently working on course materials that would eliminate the teacher from the system, starting with introductory courses in Spanish, Russian, and Arabic. Military-sponsored efforts, though well funded, have often been pursued at a distance from university methodologies and research.

University-centered efforts have not looked to eliminate the teacher but to reform language teaching in order to incorporate more authentic video, facilitate discovery learning by students, and move the teacher to the role of a task designer rather than the sole provider of information. The difficulty with a teacher- and text-centered approach to language learning is that the teacher, often not a native speaker, becomes the sole model of the language. The text presents language in a way that emphasizes written over oral forms and sometimes leaves students unable to speak or comprehend spoken language. By contrast, electronic media can offer multiple native conversationalists and introduce native speech from the earliest stages of language learning without overwhelming the learner. What is needed next is a more clearly defined methodology to exploit the technology appropriately.

Two advanced potential areas of language learning software await a more developed technology: grammar correction and pronunciation practice. Natural language processing systems have been used to model language teaching (Xerox PARC, MIT, Carnegie-Mellon, University of Maryland), but this remains an area of research with only limited experience with actual students. The technology for creating spectrograms is now widely available on desktop computers, but despite promising early work in adopting it for language learning (MIT) it has not yet been developed for wide use. Both of these await development over the next decade.

History, Literature, and Culture

In the traditional humanities core disciplines electronic educational materials have been developed in response to the demands of specific subject matter. Although no methodology has been explicitly articulated, there has been a general attempt to introduce dense primary materials at the undergraduate level and to synthesize complex materials that had previously been studied separately. In the field of history two simulations of the 1980s provide models that have not yet been widely followed. One, "The Would-Be Gentleman" (Stanford) invited students to experience *ancien regime* France in the persona of a young man trying to succeed at court. It included economic simulations as well as cultural knowledge, such as how to make an advantageous marriage. Another, "The Great American History Machine" (Carnegie-Mellon) offered census data and numerous ways of configuring it and representing it graphically, allowing students to explore many possible correlations in social trends. Interactive video simulations have also been used at Carnegie-Mellon to introduce philosophy students to issues in ethics. These are all areas in which hands-on manipulation of a simulated world or statistical model can foster the process of humanistic exploration of many answers to the same question, or many causes of one result. Despite their promise, little effort has gone into the creation of such models so far.

The marketplace is responding at the level of the electronic textbook; commercial and university publishers have begun offering literary and critical works in electronic form. The most ambitious of these, the Voyager Company, has created a format well suited for teaching purposes. In Voyager's Extended Books the teacher can prepare a teaching edition complete with marginal notes, highlighting of passages, marking of pages, automated searches for keywords, and a notebook for copying citations complete with source and page number.

With the advent of CD-ROMs some of these books have multimedia extensions. Among the most promising of the Voyager series are "Who Built America?," a history of the United States from a working class and leftist viewpoint; "American Poetry," an anthology that includes readings of the poems in digital audio; and Art Spiegelman's "Maus," a presentation of his compelling graphic novel on the Holocaust with primary documents and records of his drawing process. The extended book is clearly a format that publishers are comfortable with, since it retains the book metaphor and allows the use of texts that already have a reputation and a following. Although current software is slow and awkward in many ways, and the book metaphor can be very limiting, extended books hold great promise as classroom presentation tools and for library reference. Their use will probably be supplementary in the immediate the future until reductions in cost and the spread of electronic technology make it practical to use electronic media as the primary delivery medium for texts.

More ambitiously, several comprehensive projects have aimed at using hypertext architecture to present teaching materials. The Perseus Project (developed at Harvard, but now housed at Tufts University) presents a wide range of visual objects from ancient Greece combined with the texts of Greek literature. At Brown University the Intermedia Project of the 1980s was enthusiastically adopted in the humanities with critical webs developed for nineteenth-century authors under the direction of George Landow. When the Intermedia software became obsolete, these webs were later transferred to Story Space. The project demonstrated that hypertext could be used to model the methodology of the humanities as well as represent its content. It also raised many still-unanswered questions about the difficulties of navigation in hypertextual environments.

Most of the current work in hypermedia environments has centered on single-author collections, including the development of electronic editions, which combine texts with photofacsimiles of original texts, and with video and audio of performances. For instance, work in this area is in progress on Manrique (University of North Carolina), Goethe (Dartmouth), Yeats (University of Tennessee), and James Joyce (Boston University). Other projects (Rossetti at the University of Virginia, and Shakespeare at MIT) transcend the edition and move toward creating comprehensive electronic archives that serve both teaching and research purposes. The attempt of these projects (and many others rapidly springing to life) is to bring together in appropriate proximity to one another materials that are hard to find or not previously found. For every large project with substantial resources there are probably a hundred homegrown hypercard stacks (or ToolBook stacks, or, increasingly, HTML Web sites) developed for individual courses at single institutions. The widespread use of simple hypertext and hypermedia structures will increase the level of sophistication and the demand for more complex tools among humanists in general.

Although it is limited to text, the Women Writers' Project (Brown) is remarkable in that the compiling of an electronic archive has facilitated the teaching of otherwise unknown or inaccessible texts, although the texts themselves are often issued in book form. The Brown project is an exception to what seems to be a trend to establish archives of single male authors. Clearly more work needs to be done to make sure the electronic environment offers wide coverage of our cultural heritage and is not developed haphazardly.

The work of the Text Encoding Initiative (TEI) group has been a tremendous boon in offering standards for archiving text, but that takes care of only one part of the puzzle. A similar effort is needed in developing software for accessing these text archives, especially hypermedia archives. Attempts at multimedia authoring environments at Brown, MIT, Stanford, and Dartmouth have been either too large or too small, but never just right. Furthermore, the marketplace is unlikely to supply the kind of archiving environment needed by humanists, who require both precision of reference and preservation of context, and who also need to shift focus from one document to another (and one medium to another) as they work. It would be useful to encourage several archive/edition projects to collaborate in developing a standard cross-platform, open-architecture authoring and reference environment for humanists. Provided that the range of users were broad enough and the resources for developing the environment were sufficient, an archive architecture with multiple examples of implementation could be developed within five years. With an open architecture it could continue to be improved upon and refined with code that could be shared among institutions.

Film and Media Studies

Electronic technologies offer great promise for the field of film and media studies, but this promise is hampered for now by copyright issues. Several promising projects, including Larry Friedlander's Shakespeare Project of the 1980s (Stanford) and the UCLA Roger Rabbit project, were prevented from reaching wider distribution owing to copyright issues. As more films become available in electronic format, they can be bought separately and then used in conjunction with educational software. But this will not solve the problem of network delivery. Legal solutions are more important to this area of educational innovation than software solutions.

Teaching Creative Artists in the New Media

In addition to furthering the study of the existing arts and humanities, the electronic media are giving rise to new art forms. Michael Joyce's afternoon (1987) and Stuart Moulthrop's Victory Garden (1992) are notable examples of the genre of hypertext fiction. Electronic fiction courses have been offered at Brown (by Robert Coover) and at MIT (by myself) since the early 1990s, long enough to begin to see new genres emerging as young writers born into a world of interactive media come to maturity. Central to this effort is the perception that the computer and the Internet are not just telephone wires for carrying "content" in traditional linear formats: they constitute a new medium that will have its own structures of representation and therefore its own appropriate forms of artistic expression.

Again, teaching efforts are hampered by a lack of software development. The current authoring environments for hypertext narratives—Web browsers, HyperCard and its imitators, and Story Space—are all structurally limited. There is a pressing need for software that will facilitate spatialized writing (i.e., writing that is navigated rather than paged through), making links, and creating interactive structures without programming knowledge. More ambitiously, there is a need to adopt the methodologies of artificial

intelligence, particularly knowledge representation and agent-building, for the making of plot, character, and narrative form.

The Use of the Internet

Access to materials over the Internet is increasing exponentially for scholars and students. The increase in material on the global spaghetti plate known as the World Wide Web makes the job of humanities librarians particularly crucial. The editorial functions of reviewing, filtering, vetting, listing, and annotating sources will become increasingly valuable as available materials proliferate. Teachers will need guides to important resources and assessments of their reliability. Students will need training in how to navigate, use, and evaluate Internet resources. Software will be needed to access the many kinds of information—bibliography, hyperlinks, quantitative databases, audio and video files—on the Web and make it readily available to students. Humanities educators will be in particular need of clearer copyright rulings, and of the extension of "fair use" rules to electronic media.

The Perceived Threat to the Book and to the Teacher

One of the results of the increase in the use of electronic media is a re-evaluation of books as a technology for disseminating knowledge. Ongoing scholarship on the beginnings of the print era is helping to contextualize current unease at the supplanting of the book as the primary means of intellectual communication. A debate has been joined over whether thought itself depends upon the linear presentation and physical pages and binding of the book, or whether other modes of organization and presentation may sometimes be preferable for capturing the richness of the human intellect.

At the same time economic forces are calling for electronic delivery of "distance learning" independent of the instructor. The humanities and the arts are particularly vulnerable, with weaker funding sources but a higher level of dependency on personal interchange.

Both of these challenges call for a careful consideration of the appropriate roles for electronic media in carrying forward the work of humanists and artists. Attention should be paid to identifying what kinds of intellectual processes are facilitated by the new media. It will be important to sponsor significant educational innovations, large enough to constitute a departure from usual procedures, and to develop reliable, qualitative methods of evaluating educational results in the humanities. The anthropological approach developed at Brown for the Intermedia Project might serve as a good model for qualitative evaluation.

FUTURE DIRECTIONS

The next step for humanities teaching and learning is the creation of course-sized materials, the electronic equivalent of the textbook, and the development of new curricula based on electronic delivery of information. For instance, foreign language teaching should be rethought now that it is possible to deliver large databanks of authentic speech with extensive annotation that make them accessible to the novice. Shakespeare studies, which have long struggled with videotapes, can be reformulated once we can deliver an environment that allows for immediate retrieval of quarto, folio, and multiple performances. History can be taught with a much larger access to databases and primary materials at the undergraduate level. Now that we understand some of the basic elements of humanities educational computing, the next stage will be to develop core reference/learning environments and to reformulate curricula to take advantage of them.

The new learning paradigms will require redesign of classrooms as well, with special care to create spaces where students can speak to one another and to the teacher as well as interact with computer displays. The next few years should begin to offer us some models for working humanities classrooms, based on models in wide use now at such places as Stanford, Brown, MIT, and Penn State.

The creation of course-sized electronic curricula will require work along the other directions already mentioned: the standardization of delivery environments; the collective design and development of authoring software specialized for humanities applications; the development of new copyright procedures for digital material; the need for refining qualitative evaluation procedures for humanities education.

In all of these areas, it is important that humanists take the initiative in shaping the educational environment of the next century.

ARCHIVING AND AUTHENTICITY

David Bearman, Archives & Museum Informatics

STATE OF THE ART

The proliferation of electronic information and communication systems has created a crisis of accountability and evidence. As more and more of the records of our society are available in electronic form, users are asking how they can be sure electronic records created in the past will be available in the future and how they can be sure those received today are trustworthy. The issue is critical for all aspects of humanistic studies because these scholarly disciplines depend on the study of original texts, images, and multimedia sources. To even imagine the humanities, it is essential to have correct attribution, certainty of authenticity, and the ability to view sources many decades or centuries after they are created.

While the question of how to create and preserve electronic evidence (records with provable authenticity) has been with us as long as computing, research in this field is relatively new in part because until very recently few source materials were created electronically, and available solely in electronic form. Thus, in 1991, when the U.S. National Historical Records and Publications Commission sponsored a working meeting on Research Issues in Electronic Records, virtually no published research was available. Since the publication of the report of that meeting, the field has proliferated (see special issues of *American Archivist* (U.S.), *Archivaria* (Canada), and *Archives & Manuscripts* (Australia), within the past year), although major areas are still underdeveloped.

Currently the research in archiving and authenticity falls into four broad categories:

◆ Preserving signals recorded on different media
◆ Preserving "recordness," or the attributes that ensure evidential value, which some refer to as "intellectual preservation"
◆ Preserving functionality, or ensuring software independence and interoperability
◆ Establishing a social and legal standard for evidence, supported by best practices and guidelines

On the simplest level, archiving has to do with preserving bits. Because electronic recording media are inherently unstable, it has always been a matter of concern to ensure that the electronic signal be preserved over time. Practical interest in denser and longer-lasting methods of storing data has meant that the short history of electronic recording has witnessed the commercialization of a large number of different data storage media and media formats. The rapid evolution of media has meant that considerable attention has been devoted to avoiding obsolescence and developing methods to read and copy media from previous generations of systems. In general, previous media, layouts, and formats can be read with appropriate hardware and special-purpose software, but devising new methods to read old signals in old media is becoming more complex as media proliferate, recording and layout methods become more proprietary, and firmware plays a greater role in decoding.

Archivists, and increasingly scholars, are aware that beyond preservation of bits lies the arena of preserving "recordness." Research into what makes an electronic document or dataset a record, and how the constituent parts can be bound together, has become critical as communication of electronic information has become more widespread. In the past several years, electronic mail, groupware, and digital image banks have forced society to confront the issue of authenticity or reliability of an electronic communication and spawned much research. Most recently, research has attempted to define the functional requirements for recordkeeping and the meta-data attributes of evidence.

Electronic records are always software dependent, but the extent of these dependencies varies widely. More and more electronic objects are not merely static entities, but parts of systems in which they represent potential functionality. In recent years, dynamic links, objects that affect system states, and data entities that respond to their environment have significantly increased the difficulty of preserving electronic records. New questions are arising about the concept of migrating functionality and the meaning of interoperability. Methods of overcoming, or at least representing, software dependence over time are critical to the survival of the record.

Finally, society has responded unevenly to the spread of electronic communication capabilities. Some new legal and professional standards have been established; elsewhere research is under way to define new practices and guidelines for electronic documentation and action. Methods for bilateral commercial contractual communication are in place, but multilateral methods are still being studied. How to enable electronic patient records, patent documentation, or copyright registration, and how to ensure privacy, confidentiality, protection of proprietary information, and the management of similar information-related risks is the subject of active research on the interface between sociology, policy, and technology.

CURRENT RESEARCH AND ITS PROMISE

While research continues on each new medium, to establish its life and the best conditions for its storage and use, the research agenda has moved beyond storing bits with the growing acceptance that the only way to preserve electronic data across time is to periodically copy (refresh) the information to new storage media and, at appropriate times, to new formats. Leadership in these technical means of preserving bits has belonged to the National Media Laboratory, a spin-off of the 3M Company and the contractor used by federal projects and by the National Institute of Standards, which establishes tests for media. In recent years considerable research has focused on how to determine the right time for media conversion, how to choose appropriate new media, and how to predict long-term costs. While this research is important to computer operations, it does not contribute specifically to arts and humanities computing.

The issue of the authenticity of records, on the other hand, is at the heart of all humanistic scholarship. If we do not know the context in which information was created, and who participated in creating it, many of the questions of greatest interest to historians, philosophers, linguists, and creative artists are unanswerable. Contemporary electronic information systems generally do not create or store records that satisfy these criteria. Not surprisingly, research into methods of ensuring the creation and retention of electronic evidence is a hot topic in archives, museums, and electronic libraries. The most important research in this area has focused on the functional requirements for records. It has appeared under the corporate names of the National Archives of Canada,[i] the World Bank, and more recently the University of Pittsburgh.[ii] It is recognized in the published research of The Rand Corporation[iii] and the Dutch Ministry of the Interior.[iv] This research joins a recent thread of discussion and debate in the library community, regarding what Peter Graham of Rutgers University has called "intellectual preservation." Although this concern is the focus of discussion in the Task Force on Digital Archiving sponsored by The Research Libraries Group/Commission on Preservation and Access, at present it is not really the subject of original research in the library community.

Current research on software dependence and interoperability, which is not largely driven by archival concerns, takes a relatively short-term view of the requirement to preserve functionality. Little research has been done on modeling the information loss that accompanies multiple migrations or the risks inherent in using commercial systems before standards are developed, yet these are the critical questions being posed by archives. Little in these studies specifically addresses the humanities, except that the humanities are particularly heavy users of old documentation and thus especially need to develop means of overcoming system dependencies in data.

Margaret Hedstrom of the New York State Archives, and the University of Pittsburgh project, have led the way in exploring the social and legal guidelines for electronic records management. The Association for Information and Image Management has sponsored conferences and a task force that examines these issues; the Center for Electronic Law at Villanova University is also working in this area.[v] There has been substantial research in electronic laboratory notebooks and electronic patient records, but oddly little research has been done to identify critical dimensions of archiving for program audits in areas like decision support systems, groupware and team support systems, or even traditional "management information systems" or project management environments.

Related areas of research include:

♦ Methods for conversion of paper-based information to electronic media; research at Cornell University [vi] and Yale University [vii] are most noteworthy.

♦ Knowledge representation, including especially the documentation of archives using SGML, as reflected in the work of the Text Encoding Initiative. [viii]

FUTURE RESEARCH NEEDS

The most significant area for research in the near future is the meta-data required for recordness and the means to capture this data and ensure that it is bonded to electronic communications. The announcement by the National Institute of Standards of a proposed Federal Information Processing Standard (FIPS) for "Record Description Records" [ix] could be the stimulus for immediate research, as is the proposal by Standards Australia, based on the University of Pittsburgh research. Continued investigation of mechanisms to specify meta-data encapsulated objects [x] and capture them in implementations [xi] are most promising. Over the next five years, specifications for workgroup tools and electronic office environments will need to have these methods built in. Large-scale networks, and the acceptance of electronic transactions as the preferred means of intra-corporate communications, will depend on methods of uniquely identifying messages, controlling their access and use, and decoding their structure, context, and content. As the scientific community has come to realize, [xii] standard meta-data, grounded in a continually updated understanding of disciplinary perspectives, is essential to future documentation. Unless generic, scaleable approaches for representing humanistic points of view are developed soon, the history of modern societies in the late twentieth century will be extremely incomplete, to the detriment of future scholarship in all humanities fields. [xiii]

Ongoing applied research on the archival significance of dynamic documents, object-oriented software environments, and interoperability is needed in the medium term. There is very little active work in this area, but the potential benefits to archives would be substantial if even such basic questions as the best ways to avoid loss of functionality in software migrations were

answered. Solutions to most of these problems will need to involve collaborations between technologists, archival participants, and potential future users. Such research projects can be expected to be relatively costly and of extended duration, and will be ongoing as new functionalities are propagated. Yet unless such software independence can be achieved, we can hardly imagine the widespread acceptance of interactive documents or multimedia and visualizations within traditional communications.

Within organizations, archivists must find automatic means of identifying the business process for which a record is generated. Such data modeling will become increasingly critical in an era of ongoing business re-engineering. If records are retained for their evidential significance and for a period associated with risk, then certain knowledge of their functional source is essential to their rational control. If they are retained for long-term informational value, knowledge of context is necessary to understand their significance. Work in these areas will be stimulated by standards such as those drafted by Standards Australia and NIST in the spring of 1995.

Concrete work on social and legal issues will be best focused on identifying warrant for archival functional requirements in professional and organizational practices, locating required changes in law in such areas as privacy, freedom of information, and protection of proprietary rights and in applications such as electronic patient records, electronic laboratory notebooks, and contractually obligating electronic communications and commerce. While progress can be expected in all these areas anyway, a concerted research agenda would coordinate findings, hasten the arrival of the fully electronic society, and make it possible to realize the benefits of electronic records within the next decade. Much work on attributes of electronic business systems is being conducted in these areas, but it is currently little informed by professional archivists.

Ultimately, we must research the use of electronic records after their value for accountability has been realized. How and why are they used? What value does their information have for users, and is the value of information in records created for other purposes commensurate with the value of information contained in self-consciously created information sources, such as books and articles? What do we need to know about the content of records to justify discovering and retrieving billions of them across heterogeneous environments? What does the subsequent use of records itself tell us about the nature of society in the years since the creation of the record and the transaction it documents? Here a lead could be taken by archivists, but little substantive research has been undertaken to date except in the area of defining the requirements for networked information discovery and retrieval.[xiv]

It is now evident that we can envision a world in which virtually all records are digital, including much of the knowledge of the past. How can we make our solutions to retention, access, and preservation of the digital cultural heritage of the world scaleable? What cost-efficiencies can we achieve over keeping paper records and making them available through libraries, archives, and museums when we are deploying systems of distributed control and access spanning all records? Future research will need to focus on a variety of implementation issues having to do with intelligent information seeking, end-to-end delivery, and migration of data on a universal scale.[xv] Again, very little has been done in this area, although recent progress implementing Government Information Locators using the Z39.50 protocols suggest some of the potential for a Global Information Infrastructure locator and document delivery service.[xvi]

REFERENCES

Earlier Research Agendas/Overviews

Bearman, David. "Electronic Evidence." *Archives and Museum Informatics.* Pittsburgh: 1994.

Hedstrom, Margaret. "Introduction to 2020 Vision." *American Archivist* 57 (1994): 12-16.

___. "Understanding Electronic Incunabula." *American Archivist* 54 (1991): 334-354.

U.S. National Historical Records and Publications Commission. *Research Issues in Electronic Records: Report of a Working Meeting.* St. Paul, MN: Minnesota State Historical Society, 1991.

___. *Suggestions for Electronic Records Grant Proposals.* Washington, DC: National Historical Records and Publications Commission, 1995.

Physical Care

Association for Information and Image Management. *Resolution as it Relates to Photographic and Electronic Imaging.* AIIM TR26-1993.

Conway, Paul, and Weaver, Shari. *The Setup Phase of Project Open Book: A Report to the Commission on Preservation and Access on the Status of an Effort to Convert Microfilm to Digital Imagery.* Washington, DC: Commission on Preservation and Access, June 1994.

Kenney, Anne, and Chapman, Stephen. *Digital Resolution Requirements for Replacing Text-Based Material: Methods for Benchmarking Image Quality.* Washington, DC: Commission on Preservation and Access, April 1995.

National Media Laboratory/Commission on Preservation and Access. *Magnetic Tape Storage and Handling for Archivists and Librarians.* 1995.

The Research Libraries Group/Commission on Preservation and Access Task Force on Digital Archiving. *Preserving Digital Information*, version 1.0, November 30, 1995.

Functional/Logical Control

McDonald, John. *Guidelines on the Management of Electronic Records in the Electronic Work Environment*. Ottawa: National Archives of Canada, 1995.

Cook, Terry. "It's Ten O'Clock, Do You Know Where Your Data Are?" *Technology Review* 98 (January 1995): 48-53.

___. "Electronic Records: Paper Minds." *Archives and Manuscripts* 22 (1994): 300-328.

Rothenberg, Jeff. "Ensuring the Longevity of Digital Documents." *Scientific American* 272 (January 1995): 42-47.

Bikson Tora, and Frinking, E.J. *Preserving the Present: Towards Viable Electronic Records*. The Hague: Sdu Publishers, 1993.

Hofman, J., ed., *Het Papieren Tijdperk Voorbij: Belied voor een digitaal geheungen van onze samenleving* [Beyond the Paper Era]. The Hague: Sdu Publishers, 1995.

University of Pittsburgh Recordkeeping Functional Requirements Project. *Reports and Working Papers*. Vol. 1 (LIS055/LS94001), Vol. 2 (LS95001). Pittsburgh: School of Library and Information Science, 1994-95.

Social and Legal Guidelines/New Organizational Arrangements

Hedstrom, Margaret. *Building Partnerships for Electronic Recordkeeping: Final Report and Working Papers*. Albany, NY: New York State Archives, January 1995.

___. *Guidelines for the Legal Acceptance of Public Records in an Emerging Electronic Environment*. Albany, NY: State Archives and Records Administration, 1994.

___. "Finders Keepers, Losers Weepers: Alternative Program Models for Identifying and Keeping Electronic Records." *Playing For Keeps*. Conference Proceedings. Canberra: Australian Archives (1995): 21-33.

National Research Council. *Preserving Scientific Data on our Physical Universe: A New Strategy for Archiving the Nation's Scientific Information Resources*. Washington, DC: National Academy Press, 1995.

Proposed Standards

National Institute of Standards and Technology. Proposed Federal Information Processing Standard (FIPS) for "Record Description Records." *Federal Register* (February 28, 1995): 10832.

Standards Australia. Draft Australian Standard: Records Management. DR95194-95199. 1995.

NOTES

i   John McDonald, principally.
ii   David Bearman, Richard Cox, and Ken Sochats.
iii   Tora Bikson and Jeff Rothenberg.
iv   Peter Waters.
v   Henry Perritt, principally.
vi   Anne Kenney, principally.
vii   Paul Conway, principally.
viii   Daniel Pitti (UC Berkeley) and Susan Hockey (Center for Electronic Texts in the Humanities).
ix   *Federal Register*, February 28, 1995, p. 10832.
x   D. Bearman, K. Sochats.
xi   M. Hedstrom, J. McDonald, P. Waters.
xii   *Preserving Scientific Data on our Physical Universe*, Washington, DC: National Research Council, 1995.
xiii   Jane Sledge et al., Getty Art History Information Program.
xiv   C. Lynch et al.; CNI study team; G. Marchionini, University of Maryland.
xv   B. Hakin et al., Harvard University.
xvi   E. Christian, U.S. Geological Survey.

NEW SOCIAL AND ECONOMIC MECHANISMS TO ENCOURAGE ACCESS

John Garrett, Corporation for National Research Initiatives

> *Presumably man's spirit should be elevated if he can better review his shady past and analyze more completely and objectively his present problems. He has built a civilization so complex that he needs to mechanize his record more fully if he is to push his experiment to its logical conclusion and not merely become bogged down part way there by overtaxing his limited memory. His excursion may be more enjoyable if he can reacquire the privilege of forgetting the manifold things he does not need to have immediately at hand, with some assurance that he can find them again if they prove important.*[i]

Vannevar Bush understood the multi-polarity of technologically induced and -supported change: computing, scholarship, and society weaving an intricate dance, each responding to and in turn generating a complex web of new and old forces, institutions, rules and standards, ideas. Reviewing the settings in which these transformations occur is a requisite first step toward assessing their impact on scholarship in the arts and humanities.

This paper discusses the interplay between distributed networked computing and creativity and scholarship in the arts and humanities. The first section provides an overview of certain elements of this evolving relationship, including role transformation and agents as well as inhibitors of continuing concurrent development. The next section discusses four major uses of networked computing for the arts and humanities, and the final section identifies an agenda for further research and development.

ROLES, RESPONSIBILITIES, EXPECTATIONS

Over the last several years, traditional distinctions among key actors and activities within scholarly creation and communications have begun to disappear. Words like "creator," "publisher," "user," "work," "document," "institution," "record" have become problematic, as the activities they represent and the borders that separate them have blurred. Original source material (such as the recently discovered cave paintings in France, and the Whitman and Vatican archives) are increasingly available to all users of the Internet/World Wide Web. Internet discussion groups lack traditional status markers (such as "Doctor," "professor"): according to the by now well-known *New Yorker* cartoon showing two dogs seated in front of a computer terminal, "On the Internet, nobody knows you're a dog." The lack of status markers can empower institution-free research: the demarcation between academic and private scholarship, already dissipating in the sciences, is difficult to sustain when major resources and outlets for research are widely distributed.

Parallel transformations are taking place in the major institutions that sustain and utilize arts and humanities scholarship. Scholarly publishers (in the arts and humanities, largely but not exclusively smaller publishers and societies) feel threatened by alternative modes of dissemination (by individuals and libraries, for instance) and the proliferation of peer-reviewed electronic journals accessible on the Internet. Some of these journals, such as *Psycoloquy* and the *Bryn Mawr Classical Review*, have an Internet circulation that greatly exceeds the subscription list for many print journals.

Research libraries face similar uncertainties: budget reductions coupled with continuing price increases for scholarly books and journals have forced even the largest, best-endowed libraries to consider access rather than ownership as a key measure of excellence. But ensuring access to research information also means replacing the current library-centric system with a multi-institutional model supporting distributed information management, with associated structures for contracting, budgeting, billing, and payment. And the increase in electronic access to original material means that museums and galleries must change as well. The technical requirements of distributed dissemination and ownership of scholarly information are relatively straightforward; the institutional ones are difficult to define, and much harder to resolve.

BOUNDARIES AND BOTTLENECKS

The pace of change is rapid, and difficult to assess. Several other bottlenecks, arising from the complex transition from traditional to network-driven scholarship, are worth mentioning as well. First, the universes of discourse in the arts and humanities and in computing are fundamentally different. To oversimplify quite a bit, the humanities and the arts are about structure, dialogue, insight, and expanding frameworks; computing is about answers. Computer scientists are more uncomfortable with the World Wide Web than humanists are: it's good at generating questions, bad at answering them.

Traditionally, one must pass through at least three key gates (with their gatekeepers) in order to become a recognized scholar: complete the dissertation, be hired by the right institution, get tenure. Not only in the arts and humanities, but even in the sciences, computer-assisted

scholarship and dissemination have little if any role in these critical processes. At a recent conference, participants rejected as totally unrealistic a five-year goal of tenure entirely supported by electronic scholarship. Without movement in this direction, however, only already tenured and private scholars will be able to make full use of the power and promise of computer-supported research and dissemination.

In a networked world the lines separating creator, publisher, library, and museum become blurred. Further complicating the situation are uncertainties about the basic nature of electronically created and disseminated information. In a print-centric world, for example, the difference between an original and a copy is obvious; it is difficult to alter the text of a book or picture without leaving traces. But there is no discernible difference between an original and an instantiation of a computer-accessible book or picture, and alterations are hard to identify and trace. Furthermore, the difference between published and unpublished print works is understood; in a networked world, electronic mail (for instance) is owned by its originator, and probably (usually) unpublished.

Rather than looking for new roles (with new boundaries) to replace the older ones, it may help to think about managing annuli, or zones of progressive release (see figure below).[ii] Note that this model includes no roles, only processes. Roles bear assumptions about the

TERMS AND CONDITIONS

| Creator — Private Access Only | Private Use | Read/ Comment | Disseminate No Resale | No Restrictions | Public Distribution |

present into the future, while processes are easier to define and debate.

THE USES OF COMPUTING IN THE ARTS AND HUMANITIES

Four potential contributions of computing to the arts and humanities are discussed here: resource identification; analysis; collaboration and re-creation; dissemination. Each can increase access to information in the arts and humanities, despite significant social, economic, organizational, and technical challenges.

Resource Identification

Lycos (the largest World Wide Web search engine) currently indexes more than sixteen million home pages. By the time this study is distributed, there will be several million more. In addition, there are several thousand Internet and Usenet mailing lists, and thousands more on private systems like CompuServe and America OnLine. Traffic on the Internet continues to double about every eight months.

Currently, Internet/World Wide Web users discover resources by means of an intricate mesh of personal relationships (often mediated by electronic mail), hyperlinks to related resources (as defined by the link's creator), print and electronic directories, and serendipity.

This process is frustrating and time-consuming at best, intensified by the intrinsic uncertainties in the Internet (e.g., whether a resource has moved or disappeared, and whether it can be reached). Improving resource discovery is less a technical than a social and organizational problem, bringing to bear the skills of scholars and librarians: scholars to direct the construction of domain ontologies, for example, and librarians to generate and manage distributed subject matter and ensure access to and coherence of a given collection.

The explicit and implicit systems for assessing value in the print world are scarce or absent in networked information: peer review across a full range of disciplines; the standing of the particular publication, gallery, or museum; the background, experience, and credentials of the author or creator. Except for a few peer-reviewed electronic journals, these value markers have not been translated into the digital world: indeed, resistance to externally mandated assessment is rooted deep in Internet culture. Furthermore, librarians have traditionally focused on developing collections and identify-

ing resources rather than assessing the value of any particular information resource in relation to a specified need. What will be greatly needed are automated summarization, integration of related works into single multimedia documents, and automated tracking of the origin and evolution of particular works. As value-added services evolve, users will demand quality standards; at present, neither the tools nor the social and economic infrastructure exist to support them.

Analysis

Structured digital archives like ARTFL (for French language and literature) permit researchers to search a document corpus and locate related texts within and among various documents. Advanced programs make it possible to use semantic analysis to compare the styles of various works and authors. For some time, database programs have allowed users to introduce complex statistical analyses into arts and humanities scholarship (e.g., cliometrics in history).

These investigations are possible because the fundamental elements (words, sentences, and paragraphs) of written and oral communications are clearly defined for any given language, and carry a shared constellation of meanings. For pictorial or sound works, however, the situation is murkier. Currently, works in non-textual media are cataloged by attaching to each of them sets of descriptive words using a predefined structure and vocabulary. These words permit a searcher in a photographic archive, for example, to find pictures of sunsets, or boats in a harbor; depending on the conventions used to describe the photographs, finding pictures of boats at sunset may also be possible. Despite extensive research, tools for identifying similar pictures, for instance, are erratic and primitive; it is hard to imagine a social infrastructure and technology that would provide a helpful answer to a question like "I want more music which makes me feel like the last piece did."

Collaboration and Re-Creation

Network-supported scholarship is intrinsically collaborative. Electronic mail, for instance, permits physically separated colleagues to collaborate on research and publication. Equally important, Internet listservs help researchers identify others who share common interests, which may ultimately lead to new, collaborative research projects. Finally, networks support expanding authorship. In the last several years, the average number of authors of scientific papers has increased significantly: in some scientific disciplines, papers with 100 or more authors are not uncommon. These new capabilities contradict the traditional model of the solitary scholar seeking tenure, or the lone painter in her attic at midnight.

Such collaborations require support from new models for identifying and managing authorship and ownership. Clearly, increasing from hundreds to thousands of authors for individual works simply exacerbates the problem, but currently there are no clear methods for establishing and measuring the relative contributions of each. In fact, it is hard to imagine how such methods might operate: how much credit, for instance, should go to an author who wrote half an article, as opposed to another who provided the critical insight but wrote none of the words? These problems are difficult enough in static environments. In a networked, digital world, works will be created, revised, and expanded; new media will be incorporated; links to external resources will be generated; the resulting work may not share a single sentence or image with the original one, despite a clear chain of provenance. Whose work is it? Legally? Intellectually? Morally?

Dissemination

Inextricably linked to evolving systems for collaboration and re-creation of information are new methods of disseminating scholarly results in the arts and humanities. The proliferation of scholarly subspecialties has led to an increase in the number, and narrowing of the scope, of scholarly publications. With circulation declining as a result of budget reductions for libraries, among other factors, it is increasingly difficult for scholarship in the arts and humanities to find an audience. Artists and composers face similar obstacles.

Networked dissemination via the Internet/World Wide Web substantially reduces the barriers to entry, and lowers the cost of dissemination. For example, setting up a Web site to display an artist's works requires only a network connection, one of the several Web electronic or print manuals, and patience. And new Web sites (particularly if they are announced via NCSA's "What's New" page, for example) will be sought out by Web surfers. Absent standards of assessment,[ii] such as the institutional trappings of peer review, private Internet dissemination or distribution through a non-reviewed electronic journal are unlikely to further tradi-

tional careers. There is a real risk that individual disciplines will develop an intensified version of C.P. Snow's two cultures: one lodged in universities and print, the other everywhere else.[iii]

AGENDA FOR FURTHER DISCUSSION, RESEARCH, AND DEVELOPMENT

Infrastructure

Artists and humanists depend on a reliable, predictable, coherent, and comprehensive information infrastructure. Users of major research libraries, for instance, can depend on well-organized, comprehensive collections; consistent intellectual coherence from one library to another; and timely access to the major resources required. These systems, in turn, are supported by common sets of expectations and standards, painfully developed over many years in the library and museum communities. While certain coherent standards (such as URLs (Uniform Resource Locators) and Internet protocols) already exist in the universe of digital information, other important ones (including naming, registration, and archiving conventions) are required. Further, the distributed, centrifugal force of the Internet is not always compatible with the centripetal force of shared, consistent protocols and standards.

The World Wide Web amply demonstrates that a system dependent on URLs does not scale upward easily. URL-identified servers move or disappear; popular sites are inaccessible owing to burgeoning demand; location-dependent mirror sites are rapidly submerged in requests. Location-independent naming conventions (such as the handle system developed by the Corporation for National Research Initiatives), which are easily resolved into the location(s) of the digital information, would address this problem. But standardizing around any particular convention is difficult for the Internet. In the meantime, the standards of coherence and reliability represented by libraries and museums will be lacking for many types of networked information.

Global, consistent naming conventions derive their usefulness from standardized methods for registering digital information objects. Systems are required that permit creators and their agents to register the existence of a particular information object, determine the terms and conditions for its use, and identify which if any digital library systems are authorized to store and disseminate it. In addition, reliable recording systems are needed to allow potential users of information to identify who owns what. The technical requirements for these systems are well understood; the organizational framework remains to be developed.

For centuries, libraries and museums have protected rare works of art and scholarship from destruction. In a networked environment, however, there are no straightforward methods to determine that a particular byte stream is, in fact, the last instantiation of a given work. Culturally, it is easy to delete a message, much harder to throw away a book.[iv] Technically, it might be possible, for instance, to link any rare digital information object to a program that searches the Net for another instantiation before permitting itself to be deleted. Building a common framework supporting institutional cooperation across millions of digital collections and billions of information objects over hundreds of years will be much more difficult.

Already, recently developed digital information objects (such as the 1960 U.S. census and some early NASA data) are inaccessible owing to arcane and untranslatable data structures. There are complex technical and organizational problems in refreshing large volumes of digital information to ensure compatibility with new formats. The Task Force on Archiving of Digital Information, sponsored by The Commission on Preservation and Access and The Research Libraries Group, is reviewing these issues and will present its findings in the summer of 1995.

Enhancing Access

The idea of access embodies several distinct, potentially divergent models of technology, relationships, and the individual creator or user. One model defines a funnel from (ideally) potentially infinite information resources at one end to (ideally) a specific answer to a stated question at the other: a historian seeking a date or a geographer looking for a map, for instance. While this model may support limited interaction between information seeker and information resource, the purpose of the interaction is to narrow the funnel, not expand it.

Several new capabilities are required to support this model of access. As mentioned earlier, methods are needed for determining and attaching quality assessments to information resources, tuned for particular purposes; so are automated techniques to condense, summarize,

integrate, translate, invoice, and pay for information from different sources. Underlying these technologies, social and organizational structures are required for building and supporting flexible domain-specific ontologies.

A different model, of which browsing is an example, seeks common threads among apparently disparate information resources. Here, interactions between user and resource generally focus on expanding the funnel, or altering the course of the information flow. Tracing the World Wide Web's hyperlinks, for example, leads a user along intricately woven paths defined by each Web page's creators, ending only with exhaustion of the user's time, money, or patience.

A third model focuses on a dialogue between the user and a set of information resources (including its creator and other users); the information resource provides a framework for initial exchanges, which may result in new or transformed resources that may initiate new discussions. This model links the network as an information resource with the network as a framework for interchange (demonstrated, for instance, in Internet chat and mailing lists). At least primitive technologies exist to support all three of these models; only the second one (hyperlinks) is widely supported at present.

This model depends on a range of capabilities that are only just being identified. First, it requires seamless links between and among personal, collaborative, and public work and play spaces, dynamically controlled by the user. The annuli model of progressive release, outlined above, provides an initial version of this capability. A multi-dimensional workspace, for example, would permit a creator/user (an artist, a poet, a scholar) to manage dialogues about particular works along a path from private to public, determining at every point what information to retain, what to seek, what to share, when to talk, when to listen.[v]

Second, this model mandates seamless linkages, controlled by the creator or user, among information objects in all media. It should be straightforward, for example, to add voice or video to electronic mail; or to participate in a virtual conference, seated at a virtual conference table, observing the expressions and movements of one's virtual colleagues; or to translate speech to text, and text to speech.[vi] It should be possible to carry on most aspects of our private and public lives, choosing face-to-face contact when it is desired, not when it is required for communication.

CONCLUSION

"The historian, with a vast chronological account of a people, parallels it with a skip trail which stops only at the salient items, and can follow at any time contemporary trails which lead him all over civilization at a particular epoch. There is a new profession of trail blazers, those who find delight in the task of establishing useful trails through the enormous mass of the common record. The inheritance from the master becomes, not only his additions to the world's record, but for his disciples the entire scaffolding by which they were erected."[vii]

How far are we from achieving Bush's vision? Who will be the trailblazers? What social and economic mechanisms will be required to support trailblazers in the arts and humanities, as well as those who come after?

These questions need to be asked and answered in and through a complex, dynamic dialogue among multiple communities of practice, including individuals and institutions in the arts and humanities and computing, libraries, librarians and information scientists, policy makers, creators, publishers, distributors of print, sound, visual, multimedia, and digital information, private scholars, students, and many more. The dialogue involves speakers, listeners, and the spoken-for: all too often, the views of (for instance) artists, humanities scholars, and librarians have been presented by others.

A major purpose of this paper, and the continuing discussions it is intended to stimulate and frame, is empowering the spoken-for to speak for themselves, by finding a shared language and a collective voice. Bush began this dialogue fifty years ago, and Bush's vision remains powerful because it encapsulated technology in service to larger intellectual and social goals. Negotiating those goals, and identifying the technologies that will serve them, remains as significant and challenging as it was for Bush. It is time for new voices to be heard, and new audiences to hear them.

NOTES

i   Bush, Vannevar. "As We May Think." *The Atlantic Monthly* (July 1945): Section 8, paragraph 9, page 14. [Pagination of the HTML version will differ from this citation, which refers to the ASCII version available over the Internet.]

ii   The claim that a million monkeys typing at a million word processors for a million years would sooner or later produce the works of Shakespeare has been disproved by the Internet (anecdote courtesy of Michael Lesk, itinerant sage).

iii   A friend of mine teaches selected essences of deconstructionist theory to computer science students. Since it matches their model of the world, they find it generally straightforward and obvious.

iv   At a recent conference, I proposed the following criteria for determining the effectiveness of a global system of digital libraries: that within five years, it would be as easy to throw away a book as to delete a message. There was an audible gasp from the audience.

v   Buckminster Fuller used to tell a story about a Master of one of the colleges of Cambridge University, who noticed a deep crack in the massive beam supporting the college's dining hall. Not knowing where to report it, he eventually notified the Royal Forester, who told him that he had been expecting the call. The Forester's predecessor's predecessor had planted the tree for the new beam, and it was ready. This, Fuller noted, was how a society ought to work.

vi   The last goal has been straightforward (and elusive) for thirty years.

vii   Bush, Section 8, paragraph 2.

TOPICAL INDEX TO THE PAPERS

PAPER 5   IMAGE AND MULTIMEDIA RETRIEVAL
ROMER

GLOSSARY

AAT	Art & Architecture Thesaurus
AHIP	The Getty Art History Information Program
ARTFL	A database of French language and literature
CETH	Center for Electronic Texts in the Humanities
CHIO	Cultural Heritage Information Online, a CIMI project
CIMI	Computer Interchange of Museum Information
CNI	Coalition for Networked Information
FAQ	Frequently Asked Questions
FIPS	Federal Information Processing Standard
GIS	Geographical Information System
H-Net	A group of 57 listservs in the humanities
HTML	Hypertext Markup Language
IATH	Institute for Advanced Technology in the Humanities
ICONCLASS	A computer-based system for classifying iconography
IOLS	integrated online library system
ISO	International Standards Organization
LCTGM	Library of Congress Thesaurus of Graphic Materials
Lycos	A search engine on the World Wide Web
MARC	Methodology for Art Reproduction in Color (also, Machine Readable Cataloging)
MOO	Multi-User Dungeon, Object Oriented environment
MTF	modulation transfer function
NEH	National Endowment for the Humanities
NRC	National Research Council
NSF/ARPA	National Science Foundation/Advanced Research Projects Agency
OCR	optical character recognition
PDF	portable document format
QBIC	Query by Image Content
RIT	Rochester Institute of Technology
RLG	The Research Libraries Group
RLIN	The Research Libraries Information Network
SGML	Standard Generalized Markup Language
TEI	Text Encoding Initiative
TLG	*Thesaurus Linguae Graecae*
URL	Universal Resource Locator (address on World Wide Web)
USGS	U.S. Geological Survey
WAIS	Wide Area Information Server
Web, WWW	World Wide Web
XDOD	Xerox [document system]
Yahoo	A search engine on the World Wide Web